Conf

of a

Cataholic

My Life With the 10 Cats Who Caused

My Addiction

Marian Van Til

Marian Van Til (signature)

WordPower Publishing
Youngstown, NY

WordPower Publishing
Youngstown, NY 14174
www.WordPowerPublishing.com

Printed on acid-free paper.

ISBN: 978-0-9794785-1-2

Library of Congress Control Number: 2009934899

To Ed, my beloved fellow in feline addiction

For I will consider my Cat Jeoffry.
For he is the servant of the Living God,
duly and daily serving him.
For at the first glance of the glory of God in the East
he worships in his way.
For this is done by wreathing his body seven times round
with elegant quickness.
For he knows that God is his Savior.
For God has blessed him in the variety of his movements.
For there is nothing sweeter than his peace when at rest.
For I am possessed of a cat, surpassing in beauty,
from whom I take occasion to bless Almighty God.

From **Jubilate Agno** *by Christopher Smart (1722-1771)*

Contents

Preface: "No, I'm Perfectly Sane" 1

1. Marple & Delta: The Dynamic Duo Who Started It All 2

2. Maple: A Short, Bittersweet Tale 36

3. Dancer: Loyal and Lovely 41

4. Digory & Caspian: The Good Buddies 63

5. Cassie: The Medical Miracle 82

6. Keeley: The Big Lad with the Tiny Voice 98

7. Roo: The Ugly Duckling 106

8. Hedwig: The New Girl on the Block 119

Postscript: Patches and Thousands More 128

Six felines sunning

Preface: "No, I'm Perfectly Sane"

My name is Marian and I am a cataholic. That's what some of my friends and relatives, not swayed by feline charms, think I should confess – as often as possible – at a local 12-step recovery program for people who live with more than two felines. When I tell them there is no such program, one of those friends or relatives invariably thinks I ought to start one and become its first client; or rather, patient.

If I'm addicted to cats I'm certainly no hoarder, though I admit that when we had a feline six-pack all alive and meowing on any given day, a friend or two thought that that qualified. It didn't and it doesn't! I simply love these beautiful creatures. A lot. That's why I've saved each one from certain doom. Sane or not, I've got plenty of company (across the country and the world) in the saving cats department. "Aha, she's in denial," I hear you muttering. What can I say to that but to deny that I'm in denial?

Whatever some of my loved ones call my "affliction" (as they see it, of course), my husband, Ed, is complicit in it. Blame is always much better when shared. But no one ragged *him* about living with six cats when we had six! That's because he's the quintessential nice guy: soft-spoken, courteous and funny to boot. I'm less soft-spoken. So my critics think that I can take it easily enough when they dish out the criticism of *Felis domestica,* expressing pointedly that the members of the species are aloof little buggers that would gladly bite or scratch the hand that feeds them. And those critics think it doesn't bother me when they tell me I'm nuts because we opened our home to six cats who (they'd say "which") we daily allowed to mooch off us; plus four more moochers already gone to cat heaven.

Six plus four equals ten: ten cats to whom (or "which," if you insist) we've offered love, room, board, petting, playing and brushing, which they've loved; and nail clipping and vet trips, which they didn't.

This is the story of those ten cats – each a marvelous creature in its way – and how they came into my life and into Ed's. And how they changed us. And how each has been a creature "from whom we have taken occasion to bless Almighty God," as 18th century poet Christopher Smart put it. (See the poem on the dedication page of this book.) Mr. Smart was crazy. I mean: he was actually incarcerated for what was said to be insanity. No wonder I like his poetry. Clearly, he was a cataholic too. I'm just glad *my* friends don't have the power to lock me up. Not yet, anyway.

1. Marple and Delta:
The Dynamic Duo Who Started It All

Marple

My parents each grew up on farms. They were used to horses, milk cows, chickens, a farm dog or two and miscellaneous barn cats. But dogs and cats were not animals you kept in the house. Their attitude translated to my own childhood. When I was a kid we had an outdoor dog. When it got cold, as it does near Chicago, Shaggy stayed out of the wind and in relative warmth and comfort lying on wood shavings in the inner room of the two-room insulated doghouse my dad built for him. We also had a rabbit for while, a hen and a rooster and a couple of tame pigeons (which met their demise together when the half-wild teenaged sons of one of our neighbors shot them with their B-B gun). All of these animals lived outside. A few goldfish and a turtle could stay inside, of course. But there were no cats.

Finally, after my four older siblings were out of the house I convinced my dad that I really needed a cat, and that I would take good care of it. Enter Napoleon, an impressive all-black tom. I was enthralled. Then Napoleon got out one night, never to be seen again. I mourned.

Marple & Delta

My next cat encounter was with a brown female tabby, a kitten someone gave us. How I love brown tabbies! But she died of a mysterious illness after only a couple of years. I mourned her even more. My record with cats was 0-for-2, pretty abysmal.

It's hard to take care of a cat or any pet while you're in college. But once I graduated, acquired a teaching job and moved to Canada, that old and deep-seated yearning for a cat came back. Strongly.

At the time I was sharing a house with two friends, both of whom are also cat lovers. At a household powwow one night we agreed that we would like to adopt one of the kittens we'd seen advertised in the local paper. You know the kind of heartbreaking ad: "Free kittens to a good home." Heartbreaking because who knows what will happen to the poor things that aren't adopted? Probably nothing good.

The next night we drove down to take a look. The woman of the house led us into a finished basement. In a blanket-lined box was a mother cat. Tumbling about near her were four eight-week old kittens. Three were already spoken for, we were told. Well, that left us a lot of choice. The lone adoptable kitten was a brown tabby female with large green-yellow eyes more rounded than almond-shaped. She was immediately inquisitive; nosy, in fact. I was hooked and so were my friends. We happily took her home.

She wasn't the least bit fearful in exploring the much bigger space of our living room and bedrooms than she had yet seen in her short life. She scrounged around like a Victorian old aunt into everyone's business. She sniffed here, there and everywhere. As we watched her, amused, the three of us discussed what to name her. All at once we hit on it: we had been watching some of Agatha Christie's Miss Marple stories on public television. Our kitten would be Marple, Miss Marple, a feline version of Christie's snoopy but secretly savvy elderly woman detective. Our Marple would live up to the name, we felt sure. She loved prying into everything she encountered. But while she wasn't stupid by any means, she wasn't always cautious enough.

It didn't take Marple long to develop a distinct personality. She was, from the start, not a lap sitter but a chest lie-er. And the first of several big-time purrers. But Marple also had a feisty streak. And sometimes she could be downright exasperating.

3

In those years I was living in Canada, in the Niagara region of Ontario. Many people in our area allowed their cats outside during the day. We did too, and installed a cat door in our back door so that the poor dear thing didn't have to hunger or thirst for a moment, or freeze, or pant with heat, or sleep anywhere but in her own bed – namely, my bed – if she didn't wish to sleep anywhere else. Almost any cat naturally loves being outside if they're allowed to be.

Now, years later, Ed and I would – and do – no longer let cats outside loose, but my friends and I did then (as our British friends still routinely do). Marple absolutely relished getting outside. But at one point it was just about her undoing.

One day she slunk home, went directly to my bedroom and hid under the bed. Not just under the bed, but under the bed next to the wall. When it was time to eat she didn't come out. I tried to coax her. No luck. I talked softly to her, called her, then sweetly told her how annoying she was. No response. I was worried by that time.

Marple had never been sick to that point and now she was unresponsive and sitting in the typical "meatloaf" position cats adopt when they're in pain or distress: belly along the floor, front paws extended, back legs hunched, head low. Finally I was able to get a hold of her and drag her – there's no other word for it – from under the bed. She was obviously very ill. Her eyes looked glassy and unfocussed. I worried even more when I saw that; I immediately called the vet. I described Marple's condition and was told to come right over.

An examination and some blood tests determined she had ingested poison. Not surprisingly, her liver was having a hard time processing it. I was given some medication for her (what kind, I've forgotten) and I took Marple home. If she didn't begin eating again soon I'd have to force feed her – which I did have to do, briefly. She might have permanent damage. In fact, she might not survive.

There's a reason cats are said to have nine lives. Marple certainly did, though she surely used up four or five of them that round. She got better every day and within a week she was acting her normal feisty self.

The question was: where did the poison come from? We were always careful to keep any poisonous gardening preparations, antifreeze and oil tightly closed in either the basement or the garage. We told our older neighbors, Roy and Ella, what had happened. Ella, ever the neighborhood fount of information, was quite sure she knew the source of the poison. It had been deliberately set out by a neighbor across the street who hated cats; she had told Ella as much. And Marple had been known to sniff around that neighbor's front bushes and flowers during her daily rounds.

The neighbor insisted that cats – that is, Marple – were pooping in her flower bed. There were other cats in the neighborhood and a few were strays. But I very much doubted that Marple used those flower beds as a litter box. I doubted it not because our dear little pet wouldn't do such a thing (obviously a lot of cats would, and do). But I was sure Marple hadn't done that because she was so used to using a regular in-house litter box that we couldn't get her to go outside when we tried. Whenever we were outside and she was out too, if she had to go, she'd scratch at the door to get back *inside* to visit the litter box.

Of course we were incensed that anyone would deliberately try to poison animals they didn't like, or thought they didn't like; or to do it for any reason. In many states that's a prosecutable crime; it may well have been in Ontario and other Canadian provinces. But we couldn't *prove* that our oh-so-neighborly neighbor had poisoned Marple, so we didn't contact the police. We did give Marple a stern talking to about visiting that particular neighbor. Yeah, right, you're saying, that must have been effective. I'd say the same, except that she gave that property a wide berth from then on. Surely it was my lecture that did the trick.

Marple had instantly discovered that the out-of-doors was chock full of mice, voles, chipmunks and other fascinating, moving, edible or at least chaseable and catchable creatures. Birds were among them, unfortunately. Marple got her exercise chasing the ground-based critters and chasing ground-feeding birds. She clearly did not consider turn-about fair play. She steered clear of squirrels, having learned that they could run and snarl (and possibly bite) as well as she could. And she detested being chased by Roy and Ella's German shepherd, which frequently patrolled the fenced back yard adjacent to our own tiny unfenced yard.

When THE DOG was out and took a notion to running after Marple (when she happened to have invaded his territory or even when she was merely, literally, sitting on the fence), Marple erupted with sounds that elicited scenes of unimaginable torture. She had an amazing set of lungs for a rather petite nine-pound animal.

Confessions of a Cataholic

Marple got much too good at chasing birds and chipmunks. She began catching them. And she expected us to be grateful and say, "Well done, good and faithful servant," when she would haul them, firmly clenched in her clamped jaws, through her cat door and lay them carefully at the feet of her masters.

Need I mention that we did not brim with gratitude at these offerings, however hard-won? Sometimes she dragged the birds in alive and unharmed, though no doubt terrified at their trip in the Jaws of Death (no carnival ride, that). When I or one of my friends would grab Marple and force her to open her mouth, the affrighted bird would remember that it could (still) fly and take off swiftly. But living rooms, especially those in small bungalows, aren't built for birds; and ours, in particular, had few places that a bird could safely perch where a leaping or climbing cat could not reach it. Inevitably these poor creatures would fly toward the light of the windows and end up hanging for dear life – quite literally – onto the venetian blinds.

In the mean time, I, too, would spring into action. (I was usually the one home, as I was in graduate school and often studied at home.) I would scoop up Marple and lock her in the bathroom. Then, no matter the weather, I would throw open both the front and back doors and quietly move in the direction of the bird to get it to fly toward one door or the other. This always worked, and I saved probably half-a-dozen birds that way.

But sometimes the birds were already dead. Mostly, they were sparrows of various types (bad enough); but once there was a cardinal; and once a mourning dove. The day of the dove I had had a particularly bad and grueling morning in my part-time teaching job, and when I came home, there it lay, in the middle of the living room carpet (admittedly the rug was ugly and old). This dove had not gone easily. Unlike almost all of Marple's other offerings, this one was a blood sacrifice. It was not a pretty sight.

It was the proverbial straw that broke the camel's back. I cried. I sobbed for a long time, in fact. And in my grief for this lovely, gentle bird – which brought to the surface all the frustrations and pain I was feeling in every part of my life – I was angry with Marple. I told her how bad she was; and I hit her across the butt. Hard, more than once. Of course I don't recommend disciplining one's pets by hitting them. And only a moment later I deeply regretted it; then my bad day became much worse.

Cats don't understand delayed discipline. You have to catch them in the act if you want to teach them not to do a particular thing. Since then I've learned that the lesson is most effective when a stern command is accompanied by a well-aimed squirt from a water bottle. (My husband, Ed, and I have successfully taught all ten of our cats in this manner that the kitchen counters, and kitchen and dining room tables, are not their personal deck space for lounging about.)

As three friends in our twenties my housemates and I knew our lives would change and that eventually we would go our separate ways. That happened sooner than we had expected. We had had Marple only a few months when both of my friends left the city, one to go to grad school an hour-and-a-half away, the other to move two hours away to be closer to a future spouse. Fortunately another friend of mine was looking for an apartment. Instead, Margaret was happy to move into our co-op house on Woodland Avenue.

Margaret loves cats. She had to. It was a prerequisite for living at Woodland Avenue. We soon decided we wanted to let Marple have a litter of kittens before we would have her spayed. From childhood I had wanted the experience of having a pet that had babies, but it had never happened. Now, it *could* happen. Margaret would keep one kitten (assuming Marple cooperated by getting pregnant). We contacted other friends ahead of time to make sure we would have homes for whatever other kittens there might be. We naively assumed that Marple would not have six or seven of them. Then we would have been in trouble. But we were young and foolish, and figured we had everything covered. That possibility didn't seem real to us and so it didn't unduly bother us.

Allowing a cat to go into heat is no dream come true. It's more like a nightmare, with banshee-like screaming. There is yowling and moaning, crying, off-keying singing and general carrying-on. This is amplified at night and is guaranteed to raise the hairs on the back of your neck. Some of those feline utterances sound uncannily like a baby wailing. The bizarre sound effects are accompanied by antics that may be associated with derangement: amazing acrobatics, rolling on the floor in what appears to be a strange and painful ecstasy; arching the back, running back and forth through the house as if answering the call of some demon only she can hear the summons of.

Confessions of a Cataholic

We didn't want Marple to breed too early. It wouldn't be good for her to have kittens at too young an age, we thought. She went into heat at about five months old the first time, which is pretty normal. But we wanted her to be at least nine months old before we let her out to do her thing. How we survived her howling yearnings that first heat cycle I don't know. My mental state today may exhibit shaping by that event.

Round 2. The next time Marple was in heat we braced ourselves for more days of trauma, sound and fury. We didn't want her hooking up with just any old ugly tom, so we took matters in hand, so to speak. Another friend of ours knew someone who had a beautiful orange tom with a pleasant temperament. Orange Tom's owner was willing to offer Orange Tom's services so that Marple could produce a litter of the world's best kittens. So we made a date. But as some of you may be aware from personal experience, there are always potential problems with blind dates. And the potential became a reality. We took Marple down to the farm where Orange Tom lived. We put the nervous cats in a room together in the small barn there. Well, clearly Marple wasn't impressed with our choice of date for her. And pleasant Tom turned out to be a wimp.

He was keenly interested in her but she did not return the favor. Whenever he cautiously sidled near her she would try to smack him in the face and would then run to another corner of the room – and he hadn't even made a real move yet. That dampened his spirit considerably. The rest of the time Marple and O.T. sat in their respective corners of the room each staring at some fascinating speck on the wall as if the other cat didn't exist.

After half an hour of this *we* got frustrated – if they didn't – and gave up. We scooped up Marple and put her back in the car, thanked Orange Tom's owner (who couldn't be held responsible for O.T's bumbling) and headed home. Our let's-let-Marple-have-kittens project was not working. We'd have to consider an alternative.

Marple did that for us. My bed was her usual sleeping spot. It was mid-June and hot that year. Of necessity we kept the screened windows open at night in our un-air-conditioned house. While following her physiological demons, Marple routinely tried to run out the back door, the front door, or claw at windows in hopes of escaping to find a mate. We had always managed to head her off and slam the door shut before she got there; as I said, we weren't keen on her picking up just any mate.

One night I was awakened well past midnight by a strange scraping and thumping. By the time I realized what was going on, Marple had managed to wedge herself between the window pane and the screen of my bedroom window. She had shimmied up, with the help of well-honed claws, to a weak spot at the side of the wooden-framed screen, tore at it, popped her head through, then her body, and made her escape into the dark night just before I could grab her. I doubt I could have stopped her even had I awakened earlier. She was on a mission, and had been for all too long, to her feline mind. It was time to act!

The next morning when Margaret and I were both ready to leave the house, Marple was sitting quietly, innocently, on the top step of the front porch surveying our part of the neighborhood. I brought her inside for the day – she came very willingly – and that was that.

From then on there didn't seem to be any reason to continually confine Marple to the house, so we began letting her out again to do her neighborhood rounds as she was used to doing. Roy next door, who was retired and who spent every day all summer, from early until late, sitting on his and Ella's front porch, reported to me later that morning that he had seen Marple being *very* friendly with the orange tabby that had been making his own rounds in the neighborhood. And then there was the black and white tom who Marple also seemed to like.

In any case, the deed was done. We had no way of knowing which local feline Romeo had fathered Marple's unborn kittens. Besides a return to being mercifully quiet and well-behaved, she soon began to show a slight growth of girth that indicated she was pregnant.

Marple's pregnancy was uneventful. We had always fed her good quality food and naturally we continued to do so. The vet said she was robustly healthy. There was no hint of damage due to her poisoning (or so it seemed). As the days passed and we knew Marple would give birth any time, I was increasingly excited about the impending birth; or rather, births. I had never experienced what it was to see an animal give birth (and at that time animals births of any kind were not shown on TV nature programs, much less shown routinely – except maybe birdlets chipping out their eggs).

We read up on what to expect and we prepared a nice blanket nest for Marple in the bottom of the closet in our spare bedroom. The closet floor was raised about six inches off the floor of the rest of the room. We showed Marple the nest. She sniffed and walked away but we assumed that she, being smart, knew what it was for.

We were right. Sort of. One morning Margaret was up extra early getting ready for work when she came and knocked on my bedroom door. "Marian, Marple's having her kittens."

I didn't need to be called twice. Marple was in the spare bedroom, as we hoped she would be when the time came. That room held no bed, just a table used as a desk and catch-all, a straight-backed chair and the vacuum cleaner. The vacuum cleaner was a canister type to which was attached its hose and long metal wand ending in a brush for our hardwood floors. The machine was in the far corner of the small room, the wand propped up against the corner walls.

Marple was highly disturbed. She didn't seem to know what was happening to her. She yelped in pain a few times and kept turning around to lick herself. She circled again and again, looking as if she were chasing her tail, licking and trying to rid herself of the strange pain she felt – and the thing beginning to protrude from under her tail.

I picked her up and put her on the blanket in the closet that we had prepared for her. She would have none of it. She simply refused to lie down. In fact, she ran around the small room, yelping periodically and stopping every four or five feet to lick herself. This was a behavior we hadn't encountered advice about in any of the books we had read on feline birth. The soon-to-be-mother-cat was supposed to lie down nicely and simply pop the kittens out and attend to them, one by one. (And human observers were supposed to be wary of handling any kittens, lest the mother become aggressively protective and scratch or bite those humans.) Margaret and I were nonplussed and not a little uneasy. I began to fear for the kitten that was on its way.

Marple headed for the corner where the vacuum cleaner loomed large and motionless. The kitten was emerging ever more clearly now. As Marple did another of her distraught circles, she suddenly swung her hindquarters around. The poor partially born kitten was whipped around like it was part of a theme-park ride.

Marple was almost in the corner where the vacuum cleaner wand stood propped against the wall. She swung her hind end around one more time. The kitten's head hit the vacuum cleaner wand with a tiny thud, as squarely as if it had been targeted.

Margaret and I were aghast. We feared the poor kitten was dead before it ever had a chance to be fully born. Marple hobbled over to her blanket nest then and lay down. One push and the kitten was finally out. She nipped the umbilical cord and licked the kitten clean like any good feline mother would. It nestled against her but did not nurse. It was a lovely brown female tabby like Marple herself. Soon kitten number two arrived: bigger, male, all orange and white; number three was a creamy blue-gray female with deep blue, watery eyes; number four was a gray and white little male with slightly longer hair.

When the ordeal was over Marple rested and the kittens snugly had their first feed – except the first-born, though we didn't notice that just then. Margaret had to leave for work. I had no morning classes so I sat down on the floor next to the closet opening to relish the morning's event.

Remembering what I had read about not interfering with a mother cat's kittens, I was hesitant at first to try to pet them. I stroked tired Marple, which she seemed to find reassuring. Soon, I gingerly stroked the silky-furred kittens, one at a time. Marple didn't mind in the least. She wholly trusted me. Within an hour I would pick each one up and carefully examine it, more in wonder and thanks than to see if anything was wrong. Had there been anything wrong I would likely not have been able to tell anyway.

There *was* something wrong. As the hours went by and Margaret returned from work we noticed that the firstborn kitten lay apart from the others and Marple made no effort to include it or to let it nurse. When Margaret or I attempted to nestle it into Marple's belly she didn't respond, either to accept it or reject it. Nor did the kitten drink. Whenever we would return to check on Marple and the kittens, that kitten would again be lying by itself.

The next morning while I was away, the kitten died. Margaret called to tell me. We surmised that its rude entry into the world had inflicted damage to its tiny, fragile brain. Marple had inadvertently inflicted a deadly head injury to her firstborn kitten and then she knew, far earlier than we did, that it would not survive. So she set it apart; to die.

We were saddened, of course, but had had no time to get to know that kitten. Based on her mother's character, the little female tabby would have been a wonderful cat. As each day passed we did get to know the three others: the comical gray and white male, with longish hair (Marple was short-haired); the good-natured orange and white male; and the smart, inquisitive blue-cream female with hints of tabby striping on her face.

We were ever so grateful now that Marple hadn't birthed six or eight kittens. We realized in retrospect what a problem that would have presented. Margaret would be moving soon and would keep the orange and white, whom she named Binkley. The gray and white was spoken for by some friends of mine. We had named him Tuba. He was a funny, boisterous, fall-all-over-himself creature with a hearty meow. I can't explain why that odd name seemed to fit; it just did.

Then there was the smoky blue-gray female with wisps of cream-color. I had not intended to keep her. At that early point in my career as a cataholic I was actually so misguided as to think that one cat was enough.

Young Delta

I did name her, however; every cat needs a name. She would be Delta. Her bluish-gray fur and deep-pool eyes made me think of a delta, a low, watery land form at the mouth of a river.

Delta was the first kitten to leave the confines of the closet. Like her mother, she had boundless curiosity. On the very first day her eyes were open she began exploring. Within a few minutes she had half-rolled, half-fallen over the six-inch high threshold of the closet onto the floor. That didn't faze her. She set out into the vastness of the bedroom – what must have been vastness to her – sniffing, sniffing, testing everything with her front paws. Marple was concerned. She followed Delta intently with her eyes and then began to call her back with short meows and chirps. Within a couple of days, the male kittens followed brave Delta's lead. They all began to play together, darting back to watchful Marple when they needed reassurance.

12

<u>Marple & Delta</u>

A few weeks went by and we had found no one to give Delta a home. That lack became one of the most propitious non-events in my cat-owning career. Delta turned out to be a unique, whip-smart little gem of a cat. Later, when I would occasionally think about having been willing to give her away I would cringe. By then I would have fought off anybody who might have tried to take her from me.

At the appropriate time Marple began weaning the kittens. She needed our help, however, as she was an indulgent mother. At almost three months Binkley, especially, big little bruiser that he was, would still accost her for a drink whenever he wanted one, and Marple almost never refused him. Our vet finally gave us a sort of body-sock for Marple to wear so that Binkley and Delta couldn't get any more free lunches. That did the trick.

A month or so later, Margaret's planned move to the country took place and we said goodbye to her and Binkley. My friends had already taken Tuba home and I had begun to see the wisdom of having a second cat. Having two is no more work than having one.

Cats, I quickly learned, are not the solitary creatures so many people assume they are. They're intelligent and inquisitive and get bored without mental stimulation from humans or the attention and companionship of other animals. There *are* exceptions, and I've known a few. But in general, because they are smart and curious they need and enjoy interacting with each other. (Once of the most amazing displays of feline co-operation I've ever seen was Marple and Delta cornering and catching a mouse together. The poor mouse didn't stand a chance. If it ran one way, there was Marple; if it changed directions, there was Delta, and they made short work of it.)

A few summers after Margaret moved, I moved as well: back to the U.S. to marry Ed and establish a home in western New York where Ed grew up. In his adult life the only pet Ed had owned was a pug, which had by then gone to doggie heaven. Ed had often referred to the pug as an overgrown cat. He liked cats and was very open to living with them. Good thing. It was a case of "Love me, love my cats."

Moving day was traumatic for Marple and Delta, as it always is for cats, being creatures that relish routine, familiar places and the people they love. It would be a long day of commotion, walking in and out, in and out, emptying the house on Woodland Avenue, loading the U-Haul with the help of Ed's brother, his friends and my friends, then driving over the U.S.-Canada border to our new home.

Delta was high-strung compared to Marple, like a little thoroughbred. I was worried about how she, especially, would respond to all the goings-on, hour after hour. It would be well into the evening by the time we were ready to load the cat carriers into my small car (along with as much other stuff as could be crammed into its nooks and crannies) to head for the border. We would, of course, have to stop at U.S. Customs on our way to Niagara Falls, New York.

A few days before, I had spoken to the vet about the move and he had prescribed a feline sedative. I was concerned about giving the cats that kind of drug, and how they would respond, but I decided it would be kinder than having them spend a whole day in apprehension and even fear about what on earth was happening to their cozy world.

Sometime in the early afternoon I gave each cat the recommended dose. We soon had two four-legged zombies on our hands. Marple looked stoned. Her eyes got glassy, she sat on her haunches and stared out of her carrier into the distance. Delta looked even worse. I worried. They both seemed to have fast heart rates despite the sedation. And their eyes began to look bloodshot from not blinking. I decided that the recommended dose was too heavy, but there wasn't anything we could do about it by then.

Finally everything was loaded. Ed's brother pulled away with the U-Haul, I drove my car, with the cats, and Ed drove his car, the backseat of which was loaded with *my* clothes. He likes to tell the story of that border crossing. The Customs agent took a look at Ed, a look at the clothes in his backseat, and asked, "Do you have anything with you besides personal clothing?" "No," said Ed with a straight face, and the agent waved him through. Ed felt pretty sheepish, as he's never been a cross-dresser. Whether the agent realized the clothes were women's clothes wasn't obvious, but if he did, he clearly didn't want to get into anything with the guy in the car who had *that* kind of fetish.

We moved into Ed's small condo in Niagara Falls for a few weeks, as the house we had bought in Lewiston was not ready to occupy. Marple and Delta enjoyed sitting atop the various stacks of boxes that had been shoved into odd corners.

We looked forward to getting into our house, and the day finally arrived. This time, the move was only about eight miles, didn't involve a

14

border crossing, and most of our belongings were already packed. Our house was a modest-sized Cape Cod style story-and-a-half. On the main floor were the living room, dining room, a tiny kitchen, an office off the kitchen (technically a bedroom), and a bedroom that we would use as the guest room. There was an old-fashioned dark-paneled basement with a kind of pseudo-recreation room, an even darker laundry room, and a small enclosed workshop area. A loft-like upstairs would work as a good-sized bedroom. There was also a bathroom and unfinished attic up there. Marple and Delta had never seen so much indoor space and they set out immediately to explore.

A large yard was flanked on the south side by dense shrubbery and middle-aged maple trees; on the north by even denser and prickly shrubbery, a white ash and a black walnut tree; and at the back by a massive, overgrown lilac and equally massive and overgrown yew, and a huge white ash.

We knew enough not to let Marple and Delta outside for a while after the move. They needed to acclimatize to their new home first, get used to new smells and sights and learn where everything was in the new house – not the least, the litter box, which we put in the basement in the laundry room.

Marple and Delta adapted quickly and well to their new surroundings. So far we had not let them outside and we discussed whether we really wanted to continue allowing the cats to roam loose. A narrow flag-pole shaped extension of our yard abutted part of the property of a golf course. There was plenty to explore there, in the rough, as there was in our own large yard. But we were concerned about the road. We now lived on a four-lane road which was quite busy, especially during the morning and evening commutes.

Ours was the second property from the corner where another road met ours at a T intersection. There was a stoplight there and in busy times traffic waiting for the red light lined up on the road as it ran past our front yard. The road's speed limit was 45 mph but many people went faster: plenty fast, even at 45, to maim or kill a cat that might venture into the road. Marple and Delta had easily learned to negotiate crossing Woodland Avenue, but that was a quiet neighborhood street whose traffic mostly belonged to the neighborhood. Still, I had actually seen Marple look before she crossed. I couldn't assume, though, that she, and Delta, would understand the dangers of a four-lane highway.

Delta learned the hard way. And she obviously passed her new-found knowledge on to Marple, pronto. It had been more than a week since we had settled into our house, and we finally allowed Marple and Delta to venture out – supervised. They loved the back yard and spent much time sniffing everything, everywhere, finally covering the whole perimeter. Eventually they would explore the golf course, but that would come later.

In the front yard about twenty-five feet of flat ground extended from our front steps, then the ground sloped sharply down to the road. Just before the slope began stood a 50-year old black maple. Two more graced the slope, standing some forty feet apart and partly shading the road. Inevitably, Marple's and Delta's sniffing expedition brought them all the way around the yard and the house to the shady front yard.

I followed them around, staying fairly close. I could do nothing, however, when suddenly a hefty black-and-white tom cat came trotting from the house across the road. The tom had seen Delta and was eager to investigate. Delta, however, was already feeling proprietary about *her* home and wasn't about to let this invader breech the ramparts. She charged at him. He ran up the black maple. She started after him, climbed 10 feet or so, then returned to earth.

The tom stayed in the tree for a while then decided he had better make a move to try to get home. He inched down the tree trunk head first. When he was about a step-ladder's length from the ground he leapt down and shot across the road. A blue-gray blur shot after him. My heart jumped. "Delta!" I yelled, then held my breath. I instantly realized I was waiting to hear a thud and the screech of tires. I dreaded to look.

But I heard nothing out of the ordinary. There was no traffic at all at that moment. The light had previously turned green and all the accumulated traffic from both sides of the road had already passed through the intersection. I silently prayed in thanks and then looked across the road.

There was Delta, sitting near the edge of the yard where the black-and-white tom lived. The tom sat facing Delta and the road, maybe 30 feet from her. They seemed to be in a stand-off. I knew it wouldn't last long. The tom was likely to make the first move this time, to put Delta in her place, back across the road where she belonged. I had to get to Delta before the black-and-white implemented his battle strategy, which this time

16

would surely send Delta headlong into the traffic. The road being clear of cars once was miracle enough. But twice? I started down the slope intending to cross the road and bodily pick up Delta and carry her to safety. The tom saw me start to move and decided it was time. He charged, Delta spun and streaked back toward our yard. The big maple was blocking my view of whatever cars were there.

Suddenly, there was Delta sitting just a few feet from me, panting a little from her exertion. A mere second later came the traffic. Heavy traffic. The light had been red just at the moment when Round 2 of the feline action started. Delta was safe and the tom was no doubt gloating in his cat way that he had rebuffed the intruder as he himself had been rebuffed. I prayed a second prayer of thanks, grabbed up Delta, hugged her and brought her into the house, Marple following behind like a little dog. (Marple had been sitting on the edge of the slope, a ring-side seat, apparently calmly watching the skirmish). I told Delta that what she had done was bad, and never to do it again. She didn't. In fact, in all the rest of her life (she was seven then and lived to be 16 ½) she rarely even ventured into the front yard.

As time passed, allowing Marple and Delta to roam outside loose was creating a predicament, despite the fact that we knew with a fair certainty that neither one would ever try to cross the road again.

There were two problems with the situation. One was that they began to catch ever more voles, mice, chipmunks and birds, and we just didn't want our cats killing all that wildlife. It wasn't like they needed to eat these delicacies. Domestic cats will catch prey simply for the fun – *joy*, in fact, is probably not too strong a word – of stalking it and playing with it. That game, while natural to them, was not high on Ed's and my agenda of life's pleasant spectator sports, we being the enforced spectators.

We had put a cat door in one of our kitchen windows. The bottom of the window was only three feet above the cement patio floor, and for a while Marple and Delta went in and out as they pleased during the day when Ed and I were both at work.

But then the trophies started accumulating. A mouse. A vole. A pregnant vole laid out on the patio, her womb full of vole fetuses exposed for our viewing pleasure. A sparrow. A finch. Another sparrow. A chipmunk. Some of these were brought inside and laid on the doormat.

Others, like that unfortunate female vole, were left outside in a conspicuous spot. As at Woodland Avenue with Marple, sometimes the animals brought in were alive. On at least two occasions we came home to find birds perched on curtain rods or atop the valances of the blinds in the living room, the cats having mostly lost interest in them, and the birds no doubt still exhausted and afraid, not knowing how to escape. It was a relatively simple matter to free them, confining the cats and opening the doors as I had at Woodland Avenue.

Once, a chipmunk brought in live got the last laugh. One Saturday morning we heard Delta emit the peculiar close-mouthed meow-squeak which meant she had caught something and was about to offer it to us. (Sometimes it was only a toy mouse; too often it wasn't.) She made her way up the stairs to our bedroom. I quickly jumped out of bed, dreading what I might see clenched in her jaws. At the top of the stairs I accosted her.

She had a chipmunk. Chipmunks play dead in such situations, so it was hard to tell if it truly was dead. I grabbed Delta's scruff with one hand then pried her mouth open with the other. The chipmunk hit the floor running. It shot off into the unfinished attic, whose door was open a crack because we were now keeping the litter boxes there. (A flood in our basement three months after we moved in had destroyed it: the floors, paneling, furnace, a stereo, furniture and many boxes of books and other belongings. After we had come home that rainy evening and I flipped on the light to go down to clean the two litter boxes I was stunned to see one of them floating, Moses in-the-bulrushes-like, in knee-high water near the base of the stairs. That smelly and highly disconcerting episode had been a blessing in disguise. We now had a very nicely finished basement with new contents and everything had been covered by insurance, since our sump pump wasn't working when we bought the house and that had not been disclosed to us. Despite the renovated laundry room, we had decided to move the litter boxes to the attic.)

Delta was annoyed with me, to say the least. I don't suppose animals understand why their human caretakers are not thrilled with their live or recently alive offerings. She vociferously whined her displeasure as I shut her in the bathroom. Then I set out to find the chipmunk.

The attic had a wood plank sub-floor. The walls were not finished with drywall. There was insulation between the wall joists and a forest of nooks and crannies in which something as small as a young chipmunk could hide. I moved boxes and looked behind stacks of accumulated stuff, to no avail. I simply couldn't find it. I finally decided that it had gotten out onto the roof through some unseen crevice or other. When Delta was let out of her bathroom prison she tore into the attic and did her own search. She wasn't any more successful than I had been and she eventually lost interest. Marple had come up in the meantime. Delta, in her cat way, communicated the situation to Marple, but Marple had no success either. They both soon forgot about the chipmunk, and so did we.

On Monday we left for a six-day vacation. We closed the cat window in the kitchen and a friend of ours came every day to feed the cats and change their litter. When we arrived home the following Saturday, Marple and Delta greeted us perfunctorily. That was unusual; they hated it when we left and were normally ecstatic to see us, though they did have their little ways of telling us they didn't care, "punishing" us by acting briefly disinterested in our presence, or backing away from being petted at first.

But this was no act. Seeing we were home, both Marple and Delta very soon ignored us. They left us to go to the piano in the living room. They faced the instrument, sitting side by side, nearly matched feline bookends, waiting, waiting, staring at the piano. Waiting for what? Clearly, not for it to start playing without me. (Marple always began to "sing" when I played the piano – I never figured out whether from pleasure or pain.) Now I began to put two and two together. I was sure I knew what they were waiting and watching for: the chipmunk.

It must have been in the house after all, and ventured down the stairs, and was now hiding behind the piano, entirely safe from the cats as long as it stayed there. I told Ed my theory and he agreed. To test it we shut Marple and Delta in the guest bedroom. I slowly pulled the piano (on small castors) out from the wall. We were greeted by a high-pitched squeak and alarm-chirp.

The chipmunk bounded out and ran in a direction away from us – into the office off the kitchen and behind my desk. I also sprang into action then. I quickly shut the folding door to the kitchen, grabbed a towel, shut the room's other door which led to the hallway and put the towel under the door, since the space under it was easily large enough for a chipmunk to navigate without much squeezing. (A previous owner had cut off the bottoms of several doors to make room for the thick, green shag carpet that had filled the house when we bought it.)

I ran to the basement, then, to get the Have-a-Heart live trap. I set it with peanut butter then opened the folding door a crack to look in. I couldn't see the chipmunk and indeed it would be prudent for it to keep hiding. I quickly stepped into the office and closed the folding door behind me. I set the trap down on the rug near my desk chair and gingerly left the room.

Then we waited. Marple and Delta, meanwhile, vocally expressed their displeasure at being removed from the exciting events unfolding. They eventually settled down, however, being smart and knowing that if we hadn't answered their pleas by then we weren't going to any time soon.

Ed and I unpacked while we waited. We finished and had settled into the living room when, BANG!, we heard the trap fall shut. I opened the hallway door slightly. Sure enough, the trap had been sprung. I looked again and laughed. "You've *got* to see this, Ed," I called to him as I fully entered the room. He came up behind me but didn't see the floor of the trap. "What's so funny?" he asked.

"Look, there's dry cat food in the bottom of the trap!" I said. The chipmunk had been living on cat food for the last week, stealing it right from the cats' bowls when they were off sleeping somewhere else. When the trap shut it startled the little chipmunk, whose cheek pouches had been loaded with kibble. At the bang she had involuntarily let go of her cheek muscles and the kibble she had collected scattered onto the floor of the trap. We could only admire the little rodent's resourcefulness in the face of looming danger from two sharp-toothed felines. We were quite happy to bring her outside and release her. And she was more than happy to go.

When I opened the trap door she bounded out and bounced across the grass towards the yew at the back of the yard. Bounced is the word. Chipmunks are too small to actually run through the grass, so they have to jump, land, jump, land – as fast as possible when fleeing across a lawn. That method of travel makes it look like they're bouncing through the grass. It's comical, but I had deep empathy for that brave and feisty little chipmunk which had outsmarted our cats for a week and had lived to tell its fellow chipmunks about it.

The other problem with Marple and Delta being allowed outside daily was that they loved it so much that it became harder and harder to get them to come back inside. As time went on, they began to stay out later, understandable since most cat species in their natural state are nocturnal animals. Thus began the battle of wits between Ed and me on the one hand and Marple and Delta on the other. Now you would think that, Ed and I being human beings, we could readily outsmart a couple of 10-pound cats whose brains were probably the size of pecans. But it wasn't that easy.

If we devised a trick to get one or the other (or both) to come in, or close enough to us so that we could grab them and bring them in, that trick normally worked only once. Once! And then we had to devise a new scheme. There was the offer-meat-they-really like trick. There was the head-her-off-at-the-pass-while-the-other-person-grabs-her trick. There was the I-only-want-to-pet-you-not-take-you-in trick. And the sit-on-the-patio-and-ignore-you-until-you-come-up-and-see-what's-up trick. And the try-to-lock-her-in-the-garage trick. And even the I'm-going-out-to-walk-the-golf-course-and-I'm-not-interested-in-you trick. All of these required suddenly grabbing whichever recalcitrant cat was the object of our hunt and unceremoniously dumping her inside the back door (or occasionally the front door) at last.

This game got old rather quickly; at least for Ed and me it did. And sometimes it required heading out into the night with a flashlight to look for Delta, who had a particularly bad case of wanderlust when it came to exploring our part of the golf course after dark. Even so, she tended to come more directly when called than Marple did. Both cats knew their names very well, of course; in the house, each usually came when called; there was often something in it for them. Outside was another story. Marple was ever the game player. And only occasionally did we get the better of her.

On one such occasion we called Marple, as usual, when we wanted her in, and as usual, she wanted to play hard-to-get. We decided not to play. We called again. She sat and watched from a distance but didn't budge. So we closed the door. Several hours later we went back to see where Marple might be and if she had rethought not coming in. She had.

This time when we opened the door she came dashing in. And she was incensed that we had let her sit out there in the chill night air and had not opened the door for her on her time table. When Ed opened the door for her she was meowing as she ran in, clearly giving him a piece of her mind. She meowed, reowed and scolded. When she stopped for a breath Ed walked away. But she wasn't finished. She ran over, stepped right in front of him, turned around and yelled, "Rrrreooow, mewouwiwiouwrrr!" Which translated meant something like, "Where are you going? I'm not done with you yet! How could you do that to me?"

Ed and I both laughed out loud. Marple's intent was so clear and she was so emphatic. But to her mind, laughing at her (comic or not, in our minds) merely compounded the sin we had already committed against her. Cats, being normally dignified and self-contained creatures, *hate* being laughed at. She suddenly sat down facing away from us and began to groom herself intently, as if that task had instantly become a crucial necessity that required immediate attention and absolute disinterest in us. *I didn't do anything stupid, I didn't do anything stupid; nothing happened, nothing happened,* her assiduous grooming insisted.

Ed and I grinned quietly to each other, both assuring Marple it was ok. We understood. Within half a minute, all was forgiven, on our part and hers. But our turning of the tables on her did have some good effect. She seemed to remember that time spent outside when she would rather have been snoozing on the couch. For a while after that, she came almost immediately when called.

Besides the difficulty of getting the cats in when we wanted them in, we were becoming more and more concerned about the animal sacrifices the cats were offering. It had to stop. Both problems lessened as the cats got slightly older, but neither was solved definitively until we decided enough was enough. Marple and Delta would be indoor cats from then on. They would simply have to get used to it (and so would we).

Have you ever tried to re-educate a cat (or two) when they are used to going outside every day? Have you ever tried to convince her that she must now look at the world of nature through windows and patio doors? It takes, shall we say, a certain perseverance; and obliviousness to feline complaints.

Our approach was direct. We simply began refusing to allow the cats out. They took great exception. They meowed, they whined, they pawed at the door. They refused to cease and desist.

At that point I got an idea, and a necessary idea it was. Marple and Delta already each wore a collar and name tag for identification. And I had used leashes on them while living in Ontario when I needed to bring them to the vet, as at that time I didn't own cat carriers. So I concluded: why not get a halter for each of them, clip a couple of long leashes together and attach one set to each cat's halter, then stake the other end into the ground? We had enough room in the yard to easily do that without the cats getting entangled with each other, and they could still enjoy being outside.

It was relatively easy to teach the cats to walk on halter and leash once they understood that they must wear the contraptions. Delta adapted immediately. Marple took just a little longer. She would at first hunch down and plant her feet when she felt the tug of the leash on her halter. But soon she, too, was walking freely without being bothered by either leash or halter.

We would suit them up in the house then take them out one at a time and stake each to her spot. Those spots could easily be moved from day to day or week to week. We even used the clothesline which was already strung from the edge of the patio roof to the big ash tree in the side yard 30 feet away. Then, whichever cat was attached to the line that was hooked to the clothesline had a large area to move around in, as that line could move all along the length of the clothesline.

This solution worked amazingly well and the feline ladies adjusted satisfactorily to their curtailed freedom. Once they knew they were going outside when they saw the halters and leashes, they were eager to go. This required that either Ed or I be outside or in the kitchen, vigilant about where each cat was, making sure that there was nothing on which she could get hung up and potentially strangle herself.

Our required attention was a small price to pay for the newly flourishing wildlife in our yard and the cessation of evening treks to round up the cats for the night. This solution prevented them, too, from getting maimed, killed or badly frightened by other sources of danger: like flying baseballs, for instance.

Before we adopted the halter-and-leash solution Delta almost gave up her ninth life on one otherwise ordinary evening. Ed and I were out in the yard playing catch, as we frequently did then, both being baseball lovers. We did not use a softball but an actual baseball – a hardball, as we had always called them when we were kids.

Slap, slap, slap, came the fly balls into his mitt, then mine, then his. We would also throw grounders. Or rather he would throw them to me, since I could go chase them if need be, but he, having a bad leg because of childhood polio, was unable to do that. Ed has a good throwing arm and fired the balls down to me with good strength. Then came the infamous grounder that he and I both remember – though we each remember it differently; or we say we do.

Delta and Marple were playing together, gamboling and chasing each other. They were at the back of the yard while Ed and I played catch, which put them in an area parallel to where we were throwing. Marple friskily jumped away from Delta and suddenly ran perpendicularly across the yard toward the house. Two things then happened simultaneously. Ed fired his next grounder and Delta bolted across the yard from the yew toward the house after Marple.

Delta's head and the ball met with an alarming thunk. She fell instantly. Like a lead weight she simply dropped to the ground. Her feet came out from under her and she lay on her side in the grass. I felt shock course through me. Ed was mute. I dropped my glove and ran over to Delta. "You killed her," I screamed at Ed. I was sure she was as dead as if she'd been shot in the head with a gun.

Tough cat that she was, she was not dead. But she did lapse unconscious for a few moments. As I petted her and murmured to her she finally shook her head and attempted to stand up. Marple had been watching from the patio and came over quickly to check on Delta, a look of concern in her eyes. Marple had always been a peculiarly empathetic cat, not just with Delta, her own offspring, but with Ed and me. Whenever either Ed or I were depressed, in pain or in emotional distress she always sensed it and deliberately came over to sit with me or him and keep us company. That habit earned her the nickname "Nurse Farfel" from Ed. (It had to rhyme with Marple. Farfel was the endearing hound dog puppet that appeared in commercials for Nestlé's Quik from 1953 to 1965.)

I helped Delta to her feet, took her in my arms, held her and talked softly to her about how we hadn't intended to hurt her. Ed came slowly across the grass toward me and Delta. Of course I knew that he had not thrown *at* Delta, but in those first scary moments I was angry at him anyway. "Didn't you see her coming?" I chided him. But how could he have seen her? His throw and Delta's run had happened in an instant, at speed, and had exactly coincided in that most unfortunate manner. If either of us had tried to hit such a streaking target we would have missed by the proverbial mile. We were immensely thankful she wasn't maimed, or worse.

Delta must have had a heck of a headache, however. She lay low for the rest of the evening. But she did not act abnormal as we observed her, and by the next day she seemed to be her old self. That cat had one very hard skull, and she used up a few more lives. But there were no signs of concussion or any other malady.

Over the years since, when that incident has come up, as it has periodically, I kid Ed about the night he tried to murder Delta with a baseball, and I insist he had motive: he wanted to avenge her hunting prowess; and he was sick of her staying out late and not coming when called.

As the years went by, Marple and Delta became a little more sedate with age, as seems natural to all of God's creatures, including us. They also became somewhat more independent of each other, though they always enjoyed each other's company, and still slept near each other, if not so often curled up together as they once did.

Marple was the more outgoing of the two. She warmed up to just about anybody who would give her a second glance, and even to those who wouldn't, as is the habit of cats. They always sense whether a person likes them or not. I once read (it was the theory of a cat "behaviorist") that cats feel tension from human beings who don't like them, and so try to ingratiate themselves with such people by approaching them and rubbing their legs to ease the tension – just the kind of behavior apt to send a cat hater into nervous paroxysms aimed at making the cat back off, but mightily perplexing to the cat.

Marple was one of those let's-make-things-right kind of cats. Fortunately, virtually all of our friends, relatives and visitors either liked her a lot or didn't mind her. Since Delta was more the cautious wait-and-see type, she didn't tend to approach strangers, and so they did not have to respond to her one way or the other.

Ed admits that he had a much softer spot for Marple than for Delta. Recently he told me, in fact, that he thought Delta was prissy. I was dumbfounded. I couldn't imagine describing Delta as prissy. She was naturally cautious and more reserved than Marple. But caution is an admirable and life-preserving quality in cats. He now says he was teasing, but I'm not sure I believe that.

In fact, Delta was a beautiful, elegant, highly intelligent animal who had that mysterious, self-contained quality that can be so annoying to cat haters (who interpret it as arrogance) and so intriguing to cat lovers (who know it as inscrutability).

From birth she began to develop a tight bond with me which grew with each year. She was in a real sense "my" cat. (She was nearly three-and-a-half years old when she first met Ed.) She liked Ed but she clearly loved me wholeheartedly, and the feeling was mutual. That is not to say I didn't love Marple just as much. I simply loved her differently. As I've already shown, Marple had quite a different personality than her daughter did.

There came a time when I wished that Marple didn't mean nearly as much to me as she did. One morning in the beginning of September 1995 when she was nearly 13 years old, as I was petting her for a moment before getting out of bed my fingers probed a spot on her neck, under the loose skin of her scruff. There appeared to be a lump under my fingers. I felt again. I was sure now that it was a lump. That couldn't be a good sign. I told Ed about it and we decided we would be watchful, regularly checking again to see if it was really there and if it grew.

It was, and it did. And it didn't take long. Marple wasn't ill and hadn't lost weight but we didn't want to wait for that to happen. We made an appointment with the vet – we were still taking the cats to the vet they had first had in Ontario. He took an x-ray and did blood work. He recommended we have the lump removed but downplayed the possibility that it was cancerous.

We scheduled the surgery and the results from the biopsy came back: it *was* cancerous – a "poorly differentiated schirrhous adeno-carcinoma, likely metastatic" – but the vet still downplayed it, acting as if it weren't a big problem.

He was a big, outwardly brash man whose "bedside manner" was often wanting. He came across as somebody who could handle anything, anytime. It was a studied persona, I think, perhaps to hide his inner softness because he was essentially a soft-hearted man. But that bull-in-the-china-shop exterior could be exasperating.

Perhaps because we didn't want to admit that the situation was as critical as it was, we were assured by his words, groundless though they were. We weren't truly aware the situation was as serious as it was. But Marple's quick decline in health disabused us of any notion that the state of affairs wasn't critical. She began to lose weight rapidly. Then I found another lump near where the first one had been. That, too, could be removed, we were told.

I brought Marple to a clinic near Buffalo for ultrasound then, an uncommon procedure on animals at that time. That trip, there and back, is indelibly printed on my memory. She was a little trouper. She remained engaged and engaging despite the pain that we now know she must have been experiencing. By that point in her life she didn't like car rides much, but she didn't complain about that one, oddly enough. She sat in the back window and watched the traffic, now and then "talking" to me with meows, chirps and other vocalizations that are hard to describe.

The thought of her suffering, and of losing her – which was seeming more and more inevitable – brought a lump to my throat that almost choked me. Yes, the cancer had spread, said the vet who did the ultrasound. It was now in her liver. She could be given pain medication but we would have to think carefully about how long to prolong her life under the circumstances.

The trip home was worse. The stricture in my throat became a sob, then tears that flowed for much of that 40-minute ride. Marple was in the passenger's seat next to me this time. She sat quietly, relishing my petting her with my right hand. She nudged my hand fondly now and then – which, each time, only increased my tears.

Marple got a little worse each day and Ed and I knew the time was near to help her out of her misery. It *was* misery. We see that much more clearly now, years later. It's likely we let her go too long. But we had never lost a cat before and were hardly experts at evaluating this kind of situation.

It drove us crazy that Marple never stopped purring. The slightest touch on her head or anywhere elicited her loud purr, and an accompanying look at me or Ed with deep affection. Any cat lover or animal lover in general can imagine how hard that can be. We almost rather wished that she had simply given up, or *showed* the pain and distress she may have been in. She did not act like a dying cat. She mostly successfully masked how ill and miserable she was – as I now know cats are expert at doing. At least, I now assume she was masking feeling miserable. At that time, in the throes of that emotionally difficult situation for Ed and me, and with far fewer years of experience with cats, it was difficult to tell how much she may have been suffering, or if we kept her alive too long – for our sakes rather than hers.

The day came. As I periodically had done in the past, I took Marple with me to the publishing office in Ontario where I worked. She spent her last day lying in her basket on my desk, purring, purring. She was barely able to walk or eat anymore. But she could purr, and she *would* purr nearly to her last breath.

After work I headed to the vet's office where Ed met me, having come from his office in Buffalo. When Marple would be euthanized we wanted to be there in the room to comfort her (though she had mostly been comforting us). That was still a somewhat uncommon request at the time. And little did we know what we were in for.

The vet's office was in an old converted house, stately in its day but now somewhat dark. We were brought to an inner exam room without windows, perhaps the darkest room in the building. It seemed peculiarly appropriate.

I wanted to hold Marple myself when the moment came but, instead, a vet tech held her still on the stainless steel table. We found out only recently, nearly 15 years later, that that was because without the insertion of a catheter into the vein (now the accepted practice), veins are hard to find and the needle can slip out. That is, in fact, what happened. Dr. Brash came in with the syringe, inserted it while the vet tech held Marple, and the lethal anesthetic went into soft tissue instead of the vein. Marple writhed. Ed and I blanched. Fortunately we had held her and said goodbye a few moments before this fiasco began. We were mere helpless and numbed onlookers.

The vet sweated, clearly nervous, for once fully aware that he was thoroughly botching this delicate situation. He went out of the room to get another full syringe. I stepped forward and petted Marple, talking to her soothingly one last time. Dr. B. returned and tried again. His aim was better, but the result was no less excruciating. Marple's body seized, she gasped, her mouth lurched open and her tongue drooped out of her mouth.

Ed and I were appalled into silence. The vet and the tech left the room, also in silence fortunately, after one of them had returned Marple's tongue to her mouth and closed her eyes. Ed and I both moved forward finally and gave Marple one last gentle pat. Her fur was not the soft, shiny coat it had once been, but she was still beautiful to us. We put her in her basket, covered her with her towel then and took up the basket. Ed paid the bill while I carried the basket to the car and put it in the trunk. The sunlight was incongruously bright. We would bury Marple in the flower bed just behind our garage, not far from our back door.

But first there was one more thing to do. This will seem bizarre, perhaps, to some of you. I had read more than once that if you keep multiple pets that are buddies of each other, when one of them dies the living animals should be shown the corpse so they know what happened to their companion and why he or she will no longer be with them. This will prevent them searching the house for their friend. Cats (like other animals) understand life and death in their cat way. So we decided we would do that.

Delta had begun to withdraw from Marple as Marple became more and more ill. She *knew.* But that didn't mean she wouldn't miss Marple. We set the basket down near Delta and took away the towel. She approached, looked, sniffed intently, then sat down. After nearly a minute she walked away. We had, by then, two other cats, whose stories you'll read of in the next chapters. Maple was then about 3 ½; Dancer was almost two. Maple took a very quick sniff and left abruptly. Dancer took more time, almost as much as Delta. How I wished at that moment that cats can talk.

We went outside then, dug Marple's grave, placed her towel wrapped body into it and replaced the earth over her. I chose a rock to place at the spot. A few days later I would etch her name into the rock. Still later I planted tulips at the base of the rock. They seemed appropriate, being in their way a continuously cheerful creation, as Marple was.

In those days I felt a bit embarrassed, guilty even, about grieving *a cat* as much as I grieved for Marple. Today I wouldn't, and don't, feel that way. Ed and I have not been blessed with children. That's a major reason we decided to try to rescue as many cats as we reasonably could in our lifetime together. Yet we agreed from the start that our cats should never be seen as children, as many people do see their cats or dogs. They are cats, not human beings. But in being cats they are marvelous creatures of God, doing daily the wonderful, comic, exasperating, affectionate catly things God created them to do. And that, surely, is enough reason to value them, love them and grieve them when they slip from our care.

Delta spent much of her time after Marple's death up in our loft bedroom. She loved to sleep on the bed, or on a blanket on an easy chair in the corner, or on a towel on the upper shelf of the headboard of our waterbed. I interacted with her as much as possible to give her company. And of course she was there with Ed and me all night, every night – along with Dancer, who slept on the bed with us. Maple, while he was still with us, often slept in a cat basket in the living room.

Delta didn't seem to mope after Marple's loss. As much as she and Marple had played or slept together or near each other throughout much of Delta's life, Delta had always seemed to want periods of solitude as well. I can only guess that she missed Marple a great deal even though they had already been pulling away from each other for a while. We're pretty convinced that Delta, with that uncanny sense that cats (and most mammals) have about each other, was aware something was seriously wrong before we knew it. Since then, we've seen that happen with our other cats whenever one was seriously ill.

Delta had always relished playing with cat wands, tasseled bookmarks or other things that danced and wiggled – with me on the other end providing the animation of those inanimate objects. She maintained that interest. She preferred playing with me rather than with sedate Maple, whom she totally ignored, or with lively young Dancer, who would attempt to chase Delta and get rebuffed for her efforts.

Delta was an extremely photogenic cat. *Aren't they all?* I hear you saying. It's true; most are. But when the camera is brought out some just don't want to remain still for the split second that it takes to get a good picture. (Our newest cat, Hedwig, is like that.) Digital photography has greatly helped that situation but it can still be a challenge to get good photos of some cats. Nor do cats like being blinded by the camera flash.

One year for Christmas Ed gave me a 365-day desk calendar produced by the Humane Society of the United States for the upcoming year. Every day had a picture of a different cat, submitted by its owner or owners. At the back, a notice told calendar owners that the HSUS was looking for photos of cats for the following year's calendar. Any owner could submit one or more by sometime during the upcoming summer. I thought we had as good a chance as anybody to get one of our cats on (or in, in this case) the next calendar.

Marple & Delta

I submitted a picture of Delta that I thought was compelling. But most cat lovers have such photos of their cat or cats and there are millions of pet cats in North America. I wouldn't hold my breath in anticipation of winning. Still, I wanted to think the photo I chose was good enough to be noticed. The photos being solicited were for the 1991 calendar. Delta was then seven years old, though she still acted like and had the facial look of a much younger cat (certainly not "middle-aged," as most vets would have called her then). The picture I submitted shows her in her usual Sphinx-like manner sitting in the grass with perfect, straight posture, paws together, head erect, pale gray eyes inscrutably staring into the camera with a hint of a Cheshire-cat grin. Her blue collar and tag and red leash are visible, the leash leading off the side of the picture to nowhere.

I sent in the photo and the entry blank then forgot about it. Late that fall we received a package from the HSUS. Inside was a 365-day desk calendar for the next year. There was no letter or note, just the calendar. For an instant I was perplexed. Then it hit me. The HSUS must have accepted the photo I sent in!

I didn't have to flip through the calendar far to find it. There on the page for Wednesday, January 15, was our inscrutable Delta looking fixedly out at us in living color. Her name was in bold capital letters at the bottom left of the five by five-inch-square page. Ed's and my names as owners were at the bottom right in much smaller, italic type (non-bold). You know who was important on that page.

Each calendar page also contained bits of advice for cat owners. Delta's page says: *If you board your cat while you're away from home, get references and inspect the kennel you select. When in doubt, ask your veterinarian or local shelter for advice.* After January 15 came around and we had torn that page off the calendar, we saved it, then matted and framed it. To this day the photo has a conspicuous place in the glass case of our dining room cabinet.

Marple died in October of 1995. Two months passed and December came around. Ed and I both still painfully missed Marple's giving and forgiving personality and humorous antics. But now we were thinking about getting a kitten or young cat to take her place in the family. Not to replace her as such, of course, but to fill that feline-shaped empty spot in our lives. We began to talk about getting another companion for Delta, Maple and Dancer. That buddy would be a four-month old male brown tabby who we would call Digory after C.S. Lewis's "Magician's

Nephew" in the *Narnia Chronicles*. (You'll read of him and of Dancer in their own chapters; but first, of Maple and his odd life.)

Four-and-a-half years after Marple died, when I was petting Delta one morning my hand suddenly stopped as it traced her shoulders and back. "Not again," I breathed to myself. A tightness seized my gut. I thought my probing fingers had felt a lump not unlike the one that had proved deadly to Marple. I felt again. Yes, there it was, clearly something out of the ordinary. Not big, but definitely there. And in a similar spot.

I told Ed. He winced. He was feeling the same kind of apprehensive tension I was. We made the appointment and took her for a check-up as soon we could get in. It was *deja vu* all over again, as Yogi Berra used to say. Like mother, like daughter. Delta had inherited fine traits from Marple. Sadly, she had also inherited a weakness for cancer.

A biopsy showed that, yes, the lump was cancerous. But Dr. Brash thought the odds were pretty good that it could be removed. Which did not mean that the cancer could not or would not show up elsewhere, as we were well aware. (My own mother had died of cancer when I was 16. One's cat having cancer is not even remotely comparable to that, loved creature though the cat may be. But I knew the drill as far as cancer being removed and returning was concerned.)

Delta was as yet showing no signs of illness. She had been slowing down gradually, but she was now over 16 years old, so she was entitled. Sixteen isn't ancient for a cat; it is not uncommon for cats to live to be 18 or 20, and not so rare for some to get older still. But 16 is a rather good age, nonetheless. It's not "spring chicken" territory.

We were determined this time to do things better, if possible. We would get treatment as quickly as ever we could, but if the treatment didn't work and Delta began to suffer we would prepare ourselves sooner, rather than later, to end that suffering – emotionally difficult, once again, though it would be.

We set a morning to bring Delta in for her lumpectomy. The wait would be another two days. Less than two weeks had passed since I had found the lump, but within that time Delta had begun to show signs of illness. She slept many, many hours at a time. She seemed a little sore, and she began to walk a bit stiffly. But she was generally her old self. She had been a hand licker virtually from birth. This was no let-me-lick-the-salt-off-your-skin kind of thing. This was licking like a dog does: an affectionate, proprietary, here-I-am I-love-you kind of licking. (Dancer has been the only other cat of the ten we've had who also regularly licked our hands to express affection for us.)

This cancer was starting to seem like it would be virulent. In the depths of our hearts I suspect that neither Ed nor I were truly optimistic about the outcome, though I prayed that we'd have Delta around a bit longer, preferably a lot longer. If God sees the sparrow fall, and cares when it falls, as Jesus told his Twelve Disciples, surely he cares about the lives and futures of all the animals he created, including our pets. I had no qualms at all about praying for Delta; though of course I realized that God's answer might not be the answer we wanted.

The day of the surgery came. Since Dr. Brash would do the surgery I took Delta to work with me, as I had Marple (and as I often did Dancer, sometimes Maple and occasionally Digory). I was alone; Ed needed to be at work in Buffalo. I saw Delta to the cage she was brought to. I left her own towel with her, comfortingly laden with familiar scents. A vet tech gave Delta's tagged collar to me so that it wouldn't get lost.

I spent some minutes talking to Delta, petting her through the partially open cage door, assuring her that we'd be back for her, that we wanted to help her feel better. No human being can know how much of what we say to our cats (or dogs) is understood by them in any detail. But they most certainly understand loving tone of voice, affection and reassuring touch.

Delta sat in her characteristic Sphinx-like, rod-straight pose redolent of elegance and self-confidence. She purred and arched her neck and head in conjunction with where I petted her, rolling her cheek along my hand and licking the back of my hand periodically. At last I had to shut the cage and head off to work. Delta regained her Sphinx pose, then looked at me with clear but slightly widened eyes, that extra widening the only hint that underneath her lovely calm exterior she wondered why she was in this strange place and why I might be leaving her.

At work, the knot that had already gathered in my stomach on the way to the vet remained. Time crawled. There was no word from Dr. Brash's office. Then he did call and the call was put through to my office. It was Dr. Brash himself. He regretted to inform me that Delta's heart had stopped on the operating table. (*Yeah, so; restart it,* I remember thinking immediately. *That happens sometimes. You did something to fix it, right?*) "Her heart just couldn't take it," I heard him say. "She died. I'm sorry."

I choked back instant tears, successful at that bit of self-control only because I was as angry as I was shocked and pained. But I said nothing besides a mumbled, "Ok. We'll want to bury her. I'll come and get her after work." Later, as I had time to think about the event and discuss it with Ed – and given some misjudgments of Dr. Brash's we had seen over the years – I became convinced that he had given Delta too much anesthetic for her size and age, or had left her under its effects for too long. We'll never know, of course, but it's a strong intuitive feeling I've had that I've never been able to put aside.

I told my three co-workers who were in the office at the time that Delta hadn't made it through her surgery. They knew all of our cats and had known Marple and Delta especially well. They were empathetic and helpful, all being cat lovers, though not all living with cats themselves. I called Ed and we commiserated together. I think he met me at the vet's that afternoon but I don't even remember. Many details of that time seem a blur, lost in some strange, veiled memory vortex.

When I saw Delta's body I remember being torn between wanting to touch her, this inanimate cat who was no longer really Delta, and not daring to touch her for fear of what she might feel like. And indeed, when I did finally touch her lightly I could feel that she had already begun to go cold. That only increased my sense of loss.

I replayed over and over in my mind – unbidden, I wanted to shut it out – the movie-like frames of my last seconds with her; she sitting in that perfect posture, that subtle inquisitive stare emanating from those profound but affectionate gray eyes. Again, as with Marple, I felt guilty, and the guilt increased my sorrow. I sorely wished I could have been there before she was taken to surgery, to reassure her one more time, to let her know that she had not been abandoned.

We would lose two more long-time feline friends nine years later: not so long ago, during the writing of this book, losses which seem to have accumulated all the previous ones and then some. No matter how loved a cat or family of cats is, no matter how well-taken care of they are, and how much time one spends with them, guilt always seems to accompany saying goodbye. It's the guilt of second-guessing yourself, of wondering if something else, or other, could have been done; if a lethal decision was made too late or too soon; if the cats *really* understood that the treatment or medicines we had inflicted on them were intended to help, not hurt; the guilt of feeling as if proper goodbyes hadn't truly been said.

We kept Delta's collar and I clipped off a bit of her fur, as I had done with Marple, ensconced it in a plastic medicine bottle and put the bottle in our feline keepsake box. Again, too, we softly laid the blanket she rested on on the floor and allowed Dancer, Digory and the arrival after him, Caspian, to look and sniff. With Marple we had concluded that that ritual did indeed help the other cats understand what had happened to their house mate and why they would no longer see her.

This time I dug the grave myself. For Ed, using a shovel. and the temporary balancing on one foot that digging requires, is difficult because of his bad leg, though doable in good conditions. But the conditions were not good. It was March, still cold and windy, and the ground had not entirely thawed. Through sheer tears and willpower I got a proper hole dug next to the rock that marked Marple's remains, and deep enough to keep out unwanted animal visitors. After re-shoveling the earth over the hole I found a large rock to form a duo with Marple's and placed it over the newly dug grave. Later I would add tulips there, too; they would mingle with the ones just then beginning to spring up on Marple's grave.

Marple and Delta were the only blood-relative cats we've had, and what a wonderful pair they were. My childhood hankering for cats notwithstanding, they were the delightful duo who were responsible for planting the seeds in my soul of my very serious case of cataholism. The cats who have followed in their paw prints, whose stories you'll now read, have only increased the addiction.

Delta & Marple sharing a lawn chair in the early years at Woodland Avenue

2. Maple: A Short, Bittersweet Tale

Maple

One afternoon, two years after Ed and I were married and had moved into our house in Lewiston, when Marple was nine years old and Delta was eight – the year of Delta's calendar photo – Ed called me from the social service agency in Buffalo where he works as the chief fiscal officer. There was nothing unusual about him calling me from work when the need arose. But the question he asked me was quite unexpected.

The agency's lawyer had a cat that had had kittens which were now about eight weeks old. A couple of them still needed homes and the lawyer had brought them to work in a box, no doubt hoping that their innate cuteness would win them those homes. The strategy worked charmingly. One of the kittens had immediately been spoken for. That left a little white and apricot-colored male who was polydactyl: he had six toes instead of five on each of his front feet, making him look like he was wearing large mittens. (His back feet had the feline-normal four toes.) Was I interested in the kitten? Ed asked.

I don't recall us ever talking, up to that time, about getting a third cat, so I was surprised – and quite pleased. After asking a few pertinent questions about what the kitten was like, I said, "Sure, let's do it. Take him home!" Clearly my mission to turn Ed into a cataholic as hopeless as I am was working.

The little bigfoot was a beautiful kitten and his outsized front paws only made him more endearing. His apricot colored fur was not really apricot, I realized when I saw him close up. It was more the color of amber maple syrup. And so we called him Maple. It was a small irony that the only "American" cat of our three bore the name of the leaf that symbolizes Canada to the world.

I had long since completed my graduate work and had moved on to other things, as you've already seen. I had for some time worked as both a theological librarian in Hamilton, Ontario, and as an editor-writer for a Christian publishing company in St. Catharines, Ontario. I was able to get a Canadian work permit and to continue to work for the publisher after I moved back to the U.S. I often took either Marple or Delta or both to work with me. My co-workers enjoyed it and the cats added both interest and a relaxed, cheerful atmosphere to the office.

Now I brought Maple in for everybody to admire. It was a chilly time of year and I recall vividly that he was small enough to fit into one of the patch pockets of my winter coat. It was a convenient and comfortable way to carry him, for him and for me. He would peep his little head out to watch the world while my hands were free to carry my purse, lunch and whatever papers or books I had with me.

In a couple of years Maple grew into a large, lethargic cat. He was friendly but not no-holds-barred friendly like Marple was, and not nearly as openly affectionate as Delta. And as he grew it became clear that he wasn't the brightest example of feline wits that Ed or I had ever seen. He had nothing of the feline mental powers that both Marple and Delta possessed. I liked to think that that was because he was male. So I would tell Ed, anyway, whenever we would get into one of our lighthearted Mars versus Venus discussions.

There were two flashes of brilliance that this less-than-brilliant cat exhibited. First, he somehow realized that when the water was running in the bathroom sink he could get a drink by using one of his front paws as a conduit to get the water to his mouth with the least amount of effort. What I mean is, rather than trying to get his face under the faucet and risk getting water in his eyes and nose he would stick out his right paw and brace it at an angle against the back of the sink so that the water would run down his paw and foreleg into his mouth. I still marvel that that bit of feline genius, especially from a normally dozy cat. (Dancer was the only other regular faucet drinker. But she taught *us* to turn on the bathtub water when *she* wanted it. She would lick the shower diverter mechanism in the faucet so that it clicked incessantly until we did her bidding, gaining relief from that irritating sound in the process.)

Second, Maple figured out that if he made the right moves – the right moves included bucking and pawing and wriggling – he could, Houdini-like, slip out of his halter without it being unbuckled. Then he could lie down exactly where he wanted to in the yard, or even wander a bit if he chose (which he rarely did). None of the other cats ever attempted such an act with their halters.

But mostly, Maple seemed downright lazy. He played well enough as a kitten but as he got bigger (we were careful not to allow our cats to get fat), he grew more idle and languid. Maple enjoyed going outside but he was much less overt about his little ecstasies than Marple and Delta were. And about his agonies, as it would turn out.

By the time he was a year old he was a big cat, considerably bigger than either Marple or Delta, who were medium-sized (Delta being just slightly taller than Marple). So we gave him the optimum spot in the yard: hooked to the extra long leash that moved along the clothesline. With that setup he had a fairly large space to roam. But he seldom did. He normally just sank down in a spot he chose for reasons of his own. He lay with his head down on his paws. Or he just sat. And watched. Or dozed. Most often, he dozed. (The photo of Maple that begins this chapter is absolutely characteristic of him!)

That behavior simply became characteristic of Maple. Yet over the months as this continued and became ingrained we began to wonder. Was there something wrong with him and we weren't cluing in? Something, I mean, besides being slightly dimwitted. He just wasn't active in the way a not-overweight cat should be and normally is.

As he neared three years old this continued. He was still eating well enough, if perhaps just a bit less than he had earlier. We had always brought Marple and Delta to the vet for annual checkups and whatever shots they needed, and we added Maple to that annual trek after we got him. But nothing had shown up to indicate that Maple was anything but a slightly dozy, big galoot of a cat who just preferred hanging out in the grass, benignly, even indifferently watching the birds and chipmunks go by instead trying to send them on their way to bird or chipmunk heaven, as Marple or Delta would have done if still given half a chance.

But now Maple's increasing lethargy told me that we should take him in to see the vet again. We did, and the news was not good. He had a serious liver ailment. How he got it, where it came from, could not be determined. It was not likely a case of poisoning like Marple had endured in her early days. And both she and Delta were healthy and thriving. But there was not much to be done for him. Liver transplants for cats are not exactly an option, and had they been, the cost would have been immense.

Not long after my hunch that Maple needed medical attention turned out to be true, he began to deteriorate rapidly. We gave him the medicines prescribed but they didn't help much. By year's end Maple was a very ill cat. Early in the New Year his system began to shut down. We brought him to an emergency animal clinic on our own side of the border. He was given intravenous fluids and more medicine, but overnight he was near death. Thankfully, he didn't appear to be in obvious pain, though as I've observed, that is often frustratingly hard to determine with cats.

For the second time in our lives – and only three months after we had lost Marple – we began to discuss having to make the decision to ease one of our cats out of this world. But the end came differently than we expected. Maple had been in the emergency clinic for several days and we had visited him each day. When we came the next day, braced to give permission for the euthanization, a vet assistant took us aside. She was ill at ease. No wonder. She informed us that Maple had died during the night.

We were actually relieved. Not because he was dead, of course, but because we had been spared having to make the decision to end his life. Even when an animal is terminally ill and declining it's hard to know when the time is the right time, and it's so easy to second-guess yourself.

I asked to see Maple. This time, Ed didn't want to. I've never discussed it with him, but I think the trauma that we had suffered with Marple was so recent and still so raw that he just couldn't go through anything close to that again just then. But I reacted to this additional trauma by feeling I needed to see Maple one more time.

I looked at Maple – the shell of him – for a long time. Tears welled up then trickled down my face. His had been a short and perhaps not entirely happy life. I accused myself of having been far too long oblivious to what he needed. I didn't know if that was true; I still don't. I clipped a little tuft of Maple's fur, put it in an orange plastic pill bottle, took his collar and tag and left the room to return to Ed.

We walked to the car in silence. I cried more on the way home, but that too was silent this time. My pain was as much about having failed to help Maple or being able to help him as it was over missing him. And my grief was also for Marple all over again. It was January 10. She had died the previous October 10 and we still missed her deeply.

Maple was, in those three years, not a cat that either Ed or I became deeply attached to. Had he been well, would he have been? I think so. But we won't ever know.

It was snowing lightly, the ground was frozen hard. There was no possibility of burying Maple in our garden next to Marple, as we would have wished. We had paid the additional fee to have his remains cremated. And, for that moment, I regretted ever having said, "Take him home!" to that little pocket-sized polydactyl maple-and-white kitten.

3. Dancer: Loyal and Lovely

Dancer

On a fine spring day in 1993 I was driving along a country road on the way back from an errand when I passed the Rainbow Animal Shelter. On a whim, I slowed, did a U-turn and pulled into the parking lot. It was exactly a year since we had gotten Maple. He and Marple and Delta were doing just fine. I didn't have a hankering for another cat. Ed certainly didn't either. In fact, that possibility didn't seriously cross my mind. (At least, not my *conscious* mind.) I simply wanted to see the animals up for adoption and maybe pet a few of them.

I took a cursory look at the dog kennel, noisy, boisterous place that it was, but quickly left and went over to the cats. I've always had a hard time with all the slobbering and carrying on most dogs do.

It's not that I don't like dogs. I do, especially large dogs. I felt terribly sorry – and still do – for the dogs cooped up in small kennels. Some number (probably a large number) of those dogs are never adopted and are simply done away with. I love animals, period – though with a special addiction to cats, of course, as I imagine this book amply demonstrates. I do admit, though, that I don't much appreciate what I call yippy-yappy dogs, those little lap things that are human inventions and unworthy of any label that relates them to the noble wolf and to being creatures that sprang from the mind of God. Those annoying little critters are strictly human creations.

I was much more comfortable – in my element – in the cat room. There were a dozen or so cats there. Each made its pitch to me in its way – some very obviously, even aggressively, others subtly, and some so mutedly that they appeared disinterested, and perhaps a few were; more likely, they were simply full of stress and fear. Whatever method they chose to show it, each longed to be petted, to be gotten out of its small cage, to be taken to a good home and roundly loved.

I petted one cat after another. Each had qualities to recommend it. But I came back to one in particular. She looked four or five months old, extremely thin, gray, the steel-gray fur shadowed on her head with hints of tabby stripe. She had dainty white toes on her front paws and a dark gray tail of medium length that ended in a point, rat-like.

In the less than 30 inches of cage space she was allotted the young gray danced elegantly, gracefully, back and forth, back and forth, like some lithe young leopard, unspotted She seemed to tiptoe, to be walking a balance beam with perfect precision. She had arresting green-gold eyes that reminded me of a burrowing owl, or perhaps a great gray, and her fur color added to the illusion. Little did I know then that countless times in the future she would be told by Ed that she was a wise-old-owl-of-a-cat.

I stood in front of her cage for a moment looking her over. She sized me up too, but never stopped her dancing-pacing. When I bent down to see her better (I'm tall), she purred. This was a cat who purred merely when you looked at her or talked to her. I took her out of her cage. She purred and purred all the more profusely as I held her and stroked her. She craved the attention. I guessed that she hadn't had much of it in her short life. She looked as if she had been starved. And who knew what else had been inflicted upon her? In less than five minutes this graceful young gray cat stole my heart.

I reluctantly put her back in her cage and continued home. That evening I told Ed I had stopped at the Rainbow Shelter and that there was a lovely young gray cat there, not much more than a kitten, really. He was not impressed. "No. NO! Are you crazy? We can't have *four* cats!" he exclaimed in as agitated a manner as Ed ever exhibits. I agreed that four was obviously more than three, but only *one* more. Would it really be that different to have just one more? She seemed so in need of a good home, and I was pretty sure that, beyond lack of food, she had already suffered in her young life.

"How about we just go there and you can see her?" I argued reasonably. "If you don't like her, we don't have to take her." He actually fell for that. I knew later on that he secretly wanted to or he would not have agreed to look at her. Ed is a soft-spoken man but has a will of steel; he is seldom if ever persuadable to something he has already decided against.

Ed and I went to the shelter together the next evening. We were allowed to take the gray female out of her cage and bring her to a bench just outside the cat room where we sat with her for a while, observing her, petting her and discussing whether we could indeed own four cats without being considered certifiably crazy cataholics.

It took about half an hour to conclude that we probably were crazy, but that it didn't matter if other people thought so, and that, yes, the elegant, rail-thin gray appeared to be a fine young cat who needed love, attention and a good deal of fattening up. She had already been spayed and initially vaccinated, so that was no worry. We paid the fee, signed the papers, gathered up the free food samples they gave us and took her home.

I was struck again by her lithe, graceful movements despite her being seriously underweight. "She makes me think of a feline ballet dancer," I said to Ed, as if there were such a thing. *Dancer*. The name stuck, and proved to be a good one.

Ed loves wordplay (he's an inveterate punster). He has spontaneously come up with nicknames and little sung ditties or rhymes for all our cats. Often these little serenades occurred (and still do) in late evening when the cats tended to hover in our vicinity as we readied for bed. Marple became Farfel to him, and that's what he usually called her. (It was his special name for her; I don't think I ever called her that once in her lifetime.) Delta was simply Deltagirl. And Dancer became the Wise-Old-Owl-of-a-Cat or Dancercat, the latter accompanied by a two-phrased ditty that was a take-off on a German folk song. As Ed held her, face and belly up, against his chest like a baby (her favorite way to be held once she learned she was safe with us), he would sing to her in sweetly grammatically incorrect German-English: "Ist est eine Dancercat? Ja, es ist ein' Dancercat."

We held all of our cats in that manner, and often. If a young cat or kitten wasn't used to that when it arrived, he or she got used to it quickly. Every one of them enjoyed it. Several positively relished it, and Dancer did above all. Of course, it could have been Ed's singing that she was relishing.

The morning after we adopted Dancer she was ill when I went into the main-floor guest room to say hello to her. Seriously ill. She had a serious upper respiratory infection that she had obviously contracted while at the shelter, the kind of infection that is often exacerbated by stress. It was also the kind that caused many if not most shelters then (and even now) to simply euthanize whole roomfuls of cats which might have been exposed to the virus.

We immediately took her to the vet. We normally still crossed the border to see Dr. Brash. The fiasco with Marple had not yet occurred and Delta was equally alive and well. But now we took Dancer to the local animal hospital on our side of the border, a few miles from where we lived.

They advised getting some saline nasal spray from the drugstore to keep her nasal passages moist and cleaned out, helping her breathe. We would have to administer it every three or four hours. Cats are not fond of having liquid (or anything) shoved up their noses. (I'm not either!) But after protesting only the first couple of times Dancer figured out that I was attempting to help her. She was also to be given antibiotics to stave off any bacterial infection. Fortunately those were liquid too, to be swallowed. We could already tell that Dancer was not the kind of cat – especially then – who would have lain around benevolently waiting for me to stuff a pill down her throat a couple of times a day.

Beyond that, there wasn't much to be done. That is, nothing besides holding her, petting her, encouraging her and trying to get her to eat. She must have felt awful. She breathed noisily and licked her dry lips often. Mostly she just lay with her head down, barely moving.

All of the affection and attention we gave her was crucial. Dancer had been starved by whoever her owners had been. We had a keen suspicion that they had mistreated her in other ways, as she was wary at first of close contact and lashed out with claws or teeth if startled, or if I

44

petted her too long – though she desperately needed that contact. We called the shelter, too, and told them about Dancer being ill. They didn't react much, though asked if we wanted to return her. No, we didn't. But I asked, nevertheless, "What will happen to her if we return her?" In a less-than straightforward manner we were given the message that she wouldn't make it. They would not be nursing her back to health.

We did briefly wonder whether we could keep Dancer. That first afternoon while I sat with her in my lap *I* began to have difficulty breathing. I have asthma and my bronchial tubes felt like they were seizing up. Then my nose became congested. I laid Dancer in her bed, took a hit on my emergency asthma inhaler, then began to wonder what else I could do – for myself, this time, since my inhaler didn't seem to be having much affect.

I drank some strong black coffee, a natural bronchodilator, and considered how to proceed. Returning Dancer to the shelter would mean her certain death. I had already washed my hands thoroughly after having tended to her and laying her down. I then changed both my jeans and my blouse and put them in the wash to get away from and rid of her dander, which was likely causing my reaction. (I had never reacted like that to Marple, Delta or Maple.) I gradually began to breathe more easily once I had washed my hands and changed my clothes.

When it was time once more for Dancer's nose drops and medicine, I brought a nicely warm, damp, but well wrung-out washcloth and a couple of towels with me. Before picking her up I ran the washcloth across her head, back and paws to trap loose dander. I put a towel over my chest and shoulders and one on my lap. It was my version of a hazard suit. Then Ed handed Dancer to me. I tended, held and petted her as usual, but now with my clothing protected by the towels. When I laid her down again I carefully folded the towels then washed my face, hands and lower arms with hot, soapy water.

The next day was better, for both Dancer and me. And the next day better still. By the end of the week Dancer was showing signs of being the active, inquisitive cat we thought we had adopted and I was breathing normally. I never again had a problem with an allergic reaction to Dancer – nor to any cats that arrived subsequently.

Because Dancer was immediately sick after we brought her home we didn't go through the same semi-isolation procedure we had followed when we introduced Maple to Marple and Delta. Dancer was already in semi-isolation in our guest room, and we closed the door each night so that she was mostly unaware of the other cats. Nor did they have a chance to react to her as an intruder. When Maple arrived we had kept him in that same room for a couple of days, where he and Marple and Delta could sniff each other under the door but not bother – or fight – with each other. Being just eight-weeks old he wasn't perceived as a threat by either older cat, and he was accepted by them quite quickly.

Dancer was a bit older so the introduction, especially to Marple and Delta, might be more of a challenge. Add to that the fact that she was also skittish about "her" space being invaded. Once Dancer started nosing under the door and the other cats became aware of her presence, the final introduction of her to the others was only a day or two away. In the event, it went well. Soon, little Dancer, thoroughly recovered, had decided that her favorite pastime was to run after the older cats, especially Marple, no doubt in hopes of getting them to play.

Dancer didn't just run after Marple briefly then give up; she lay in wait for her, hiding around corners, behind doors and crouching below the top step of the basement stairs (that stairway had no closable door). At precisely the right moment Dancer would jump out at Marple and the chase would be on. I thought of a crazy silent-film cops-and-robbers chase – except for the silent part! Marple would yowl and scream as if being tortured. Had our neighbors been close enough to hear, they may well have thought we were animal abusers and reported us to the police.

Marple's vocal carrying on was almost entirely for effect, meant to impress or scare young Dancer into submission. But after the first time or two this strategy didn't work. Dancer was smart. But Marple continued her torturous caterwauling anyway. Then Dancer would pounce, Marple would jump out of the way and the chase would continue another round or two. Occasionally Dancer would hit her target. (I suspect that most of the time she deliberately did not. She did have *some* respect for Marple's experience and potential to discipline her into subjection.)

If she actually landed on Marple, or close enough to touch her, there would be a brief brawl or boxing match – with continued impressive sound effects, to be sure. But such fights were of a mostly benign variety. Dancer did not outgrow her love for this game. And since Marple continued to allow it, we suspected that Marple didn't either, despite her vocal protestations otherwise. Delta, however, took it seriously, and Dancer learned very quickly that Delta did not consider it a game. After just a couple of tries with Delta, Dancer backed off, left Delta in peace and concentrated her efforts from then on on Marple alone. Maple, being not quite a year older than Dancer, was a different kind of playmate: a male buddy and an equal. They would roll around together and frequently sleep curled up together.

One of the best examples of turn-about-is-fair-play Ed and I ever saw in our career as cataholics was this: when Dancer was about three years old and Digory came on the scene after Marple died, Digory instinctively initiated Dancer's game. His target was Dancer herself. Digory would lie in wait for her using exactly the tactics Dancer had developed against Marple. And Dancer would yowl and scream and hiss even more impressively than Marple had. But Dancer wasn't quite as good-natured about letting Digory catch her. She preferred that this young upstart keep his silly game to himself. She had a short memory.

As Marple and Delta became teenagers in actual years I did not bring them to work with me nearly as often as I had previously. Part of the reason was that they gradually began to dislike the car ride. Perhaps they too much associated it with going to the vet.

I began to take Dancer with me instead. I didn't put her in a carrier. I didn't need to. I had a small car, a sub-compact, and she would occupy the passenger seat next to me, the very model of a perfect passenger. She would sit Delta-Sphinx-like, looking out the front window. Or she would turn and look out the side window. She seemed both puzzled and fascinated by how fast the scenery whizzed by. Now and then she would stand on her hind legs, her front paws resting at the bottom edge of the window to get a better view.

I would talk to her, or sing to her; or sing to her along with the radio – though I almost always listened to classical music and what was most often played was not vocal or choral music. I wasn't into the Top 40 and so Dancer wasn't.

All of our cats have been soothed by classical music. They have all gathered around the piano when I play, though if I also sang Marple would jump up on the bench, then the keyboard and put her face up near mine, meowing loudly, as if trying to sing a duet with me. Maybe she just hoped that I'd shut up.

Once in a while Dancer would head to the back seat, then jump into the back window and lie down there to survey the receding landscape, much to the interest and delight of my fellow motorists. That, however, was more often Digory's preferred spot when he was the one I took to work (along with Caspian). After we got Caspian, and Digory and Caspian became best buddies, I tended to take either them together or Dancer alone to work with me.

Crossing the U.S.-Canada border with a cat or two in the car was fun. (For some years after Ed and I married and began our life together in western New York I continued to work in Ontario.) There was no problem taking the cats into Canada. The only requirement was that they have up-to-date rabies shots, which we made sure they always did, and which little cards listing their vaccinations proved.

Almost all of the Customs officers from both countries – the Canadians on the way to work, the Americans on the way home – were happy to see the cats. In fact, if now and then I didn't happen to have at least one cat with me when I crossed the border, the agents almost always asked, "Where are the cats today?" The cats provided a few moments of lightness and out-of-the-ordinary interest for the agents.

The agents became noticeably more free, talkative and overtly friendly if I had a cat with me in the car. Not that most of the agents were normally unfriendly, but the phenomenon is well known. Strangers or people known to you only by sight are much more likely to react in a friendly greeting or in some other openly cordial manner if you are accompanied by an animal (or two). And if I were holding Dancer or Digory, as I usually did once I had rolled down the window to talk with the agent, that agent might very well reach out a hand to give the cat a pat and ask its name.

Of the ten cats we've had so far, Dancer gradually became the one most wholeheartedly committed to us as her keepers and "masters." She came to trust us completely and irrevocably. She especially trusted me, as I had more intimate day-to-day, even hour-to-hour, interaction with her in her lifetime than Ed was able to have.

That deep commitment to us is perhaps remarkable in light of her initial tendency to lash out violently when something didn't go her way, or if she felt the least bit confined or restrained when she did not wish to be. Early on, I had to be extremely careful, for instance, how I went about putting her into her halter and leash when she went outside with the other cats. She would not tolerate being messed with for more than minimal seconds. If, in that amount of time, I hadn't managed to slip the already buckled upper loop of her halter over her head, then buckled the lower loop around her belly as well, I had better watch out for my hands. I was likely to come away with scratches.

Over the years, however, those very frequent states of high-alert gradually diminished, as did their severity. She became ever more tolerant as she aged. She always kept a mind of her own – what self-respecting cat does not? But she learned that in our household no bad thing would come to cats who wait.

The spring of 2000 was busy – and both painful and exciting. In March we went through the grief of Delta's death. In April I resigned my 16-year editorship in Ontario to begin freelancing and writing my first book (a biography of composer George Frideric Handel). That career change was good, creatively and emotionally if not financially. But it was a bigger change than I had expected, even though I was working in the same field. Therefore it was initially traumatic. I took a welcome break before I began lining up freelance work and researching my book by making a trip to Britain for the first time to visit friends there. (Ed wasn't able to go, but the very next year he and I would have an opportunity to make the same trip together.)

Losing Delta was heartbreaking, but we had to turn our attention to the care of our remaining cats, Dancer, Digory and Caspian. Digory arrived two months after Marple's death, Caspian just after Maple died. A year later we unexpectedly adopted Cassie. Dancer was by then the old hand of the group, having come to us seven years earlier. She continued to delight, amuse and amaze us.

Having become so immediately and intimately attached to me, and only slightly less so to Ed, she was a bit wary of strangers who came into the house. When the doorbell would ring she vamoosed. "Better to be safe than sorry" was her proverbial motto. But then, when she had determined that whoever or whatever was at the door was no threat, she would re-emerge and act the winsome little lady that we knew she was. The exception was when construction workers were in the house day after day renovating our kitchen. That was not a bit to her liking, and the other cats didn't like it much either, yet *their* curiosity tended to get the better of them. Not Dancer. The men made far too much racket to suit her. Nor was she impressed with their periodic attempts to seduce her into coming close enough to be petted. She decided that the quietest, safest place to stay for the duration was upstairs, and so she camped out on our bed for days until the unwanted visitors finally left.

Dancer was not a wimp or a fraidy cat; she was merely cautious until she had sized up a new person, persons or situation. She had quickly adapted to my co-workers at the publishing office and was happy on the mornings when I would scoop her up in one arm, my purse, books or lunch in the other, and head to the garage. She loved the ride, and relished being the Only Cat for the duration of the work day.

She spent most of those days lying on my desk or a chair, but she would also wander out to visit my co-workers. She particularly liked our daily morning coffee break. No, unlike her owners she was not a coffee addict, but she loved to participate by sitting on my lap, watching and listening. Now and then she would be offered a tiny puddle of cream in a saucer, well worth jumping off my lap to get. And she gobbled up morsels of muffin with butter or bite-sized bits of Tim Horton's old-fashioned plain donuts, her favorite and mine.

While in my lap, sitting up straight, she was just tall enough for her head to reach over the top of the table, a sight that made us smile and that always elicited chuckling comments from visitors. If I would pull back from the table, having finished my coffee and snack, I would cross my legs and she would lie along the length of my upper leg facing the table, her front paws and face at my knee.

What was fascinating about Dancer's coffee break routine was that she was never otherwise a lap sitter. She adored being petted, talked to and interacted with in any way, and was our only cat who always purred at even the slightest verbal provocation; there was no need to even touch her to get her motor going. But she didn't seek out laps. Who knows what is in the mind of a cat, or why in certain circumstances they deviate from routine, though they are the ultimate creatures of habit?

Every year the publication I worked for put out a Christmas issue.

Dancer

One year, when Dancer had been a regular at the office she was included in that issue. There was always a Christmas greeting to readers from the staff. That year, along with that greeting there was a group photo. Identifying each person was a facsimile of his or her signature. In the photo, I was holding Dancer, who was even more amazingly photogenic than Delta was. Below my picture was my signature; next to that was Dancer's: an inked imprint of her right front paw. Not surprisingly, we received many bemused comments on that photo.

Dancer adjusted well to the arrival of Digory, Caspian, Cassie, and later Keeley and Roo, in their turn. But after Marple and Delta were gone she never again warmed up to another of her own kind as she had as a kitten to Maple, to Marple, and tried to do with Delta. She would be among the intent feline crowd that gathered around the patio doors when a chipmunk, squirrel or small flock of sparrows just outside the doors were searching here and there for seeds. And she of course was among the crowd when it was chow time twice a day. But she mostly kept her own counsel and did her own thing. Every feline newcomer, in turn, found out that Dancer could be friendly enough but was not to be messed with. She had her own likes and dislikes, and one of those dislikes was any other cat getting in her face. She was the matriarch, and what the matriarch wanted, the "kids" had better comply with.

Of all of Dancer's feline house mates, however, Digory, was slow to get the hint. He continued (biding his time), to deliberately annoy Dancer. Digory, as I said earlier, began, at his arrival when Dancer was almost three, to give Dancer the same medicine she had delighted in giving Marple.

Gradually he backed off as Dancer belted him across the face a few too many times (always accompanied by wildcat sound effects). But at regular intervals over the years, even when Dancer was past 16, he just couldn't seem to help himself. He would periodically go after her, waiting to ambush her as of old. Such forays on Digory's part seemed not entirely motivated by goodness and light. They were payback for Dancer's discipline of him, perhaps. His intent was always clear (he would periodically pick fights with Keeley as well).

While Digory has some lovely traits he's the only cat we've had that has a genuine jealous streak that he sometimes directs against one of the other cats (more of that in his chapter). Because of Digory's volatility and unpredictability, Dancer did not sleep on our bed in the winter when the other cats snuggled down together there. She just didn't want to be that close to Digory. She was uneasy about what he might do if they got in too close proximity to each other. That changed after we moved. On Good Friday of 2005 we moved to a ranch-style house in the next town, less than 10- miles from where we had lived for the previous 15 years. Within a week of the move, Dancer made her own move that both surprised and pleased me immensely. I sleep with an additional pillow (under the blankets) on my side, at the outer edge of the bed. The weather was still chilly; cold, in fact, but we turn down the heat quite drastically at night. So it was still pile-on-the-bed-season for the cats.

Suddenly, there was Dancer. She nestled into the pillow next to me, on top of the blankets but close enough for me to feel her body heat, and she mine. From then on and for the rest of her life Dancer slept at least part of every night next to me on the bed. She seemed to have decided, after so many years, that that was simply what she wanted and it didn't matter what Digory did or "said"; or where he happened to be on the bed (though she still preferred that he not be too close). Some message must have passed between Dancer and Digory because he never again harassed her. He finally seemed to have understood that Dancer was the elder among them and deserved respect.

Life went on happily for Dancer. She was well into her teens now, but she was still kittenishly playful in many respects. And she remained the instant purrer. As older cats do, however, she began to get a little stiff, particularly in the rear left leg. She was developing a bit of arthritis. We began regularly giving her a natural remedy for it – a feline version of the glucosamine and condroitin that helped my own joint aches. After a while she began to slow down some and to eat a bit less. We bought a low stool for her to help her jump onto the bed more easily. We wondered now and then how long we would have her with us.

Ed had concocted a wonderful little story about a fictional alter-ego of Dancer's, or perhaps an ancient royal ancestor of hers. He would tell her the story and add to it periodically (the story was for meant for me, of course, but he would direct it at Dancer herself).

The alter-ego/ancestor was named Stute Naglia (pronounced Nay-glia) of Old. (Or Stupe Naglia – Ed and I had a good-natured ongoing disagreement about that, the "historical record" being uncertain. Where

52

either name came from remains a mystery!) Stupe Naglia lived back in the 17th century, around the time of the Jamestown settlement in America (1607). In our hallway hangs a woodcut of a cat from that time. That, Ed decided, was Stupe Naglia's portrait. So in January 2007 Dancer would celebrate the quadricentennial of Stupe Naglia of Old. But we began to wonder if Dancer would see that quadricentennial as she seemed to become a bit more frail over time. However, as she had often in her long life, she surprised us. She was not only alive but quite well when 2007 came around. We enjoyed every passing week and month with Dancer in our now large feline family of six.

About two years later, at Thanksgiving 2008, Dancer reached a crisis. It had recently been getting difficult to get her to eat. I had to follow her around with her food bowl. She would become easily distracted and seemingly forget to finish her food. Then Caspian and Keeley, large piggy males that they are, would quickly move in to gulp down the rest.

One morning Dancer wouldn't eat at all. It was the Saturday of Thanksgiving weekend. We had for some time been bringing the cats to an excellent young vet on our side of the border who had opened his own clinic a few years earlier. He had state-of-the-art facilities, but the clinic wasn't open on that Saturday.

We would have to bring Dancer to an emergency clinic instead. We called and they told us to bring her right in. That clinic vet guessed that Dancer was experiencing kidney failure. She was definitely dehydrated. Blood tests would be taken but even before the results were known it would be crucial for her to stay there and be given intravenous fluids and electrolytes. We reluctantly said goodbye to Dancer and left. The expense for three days in the hospital and all that came with it would be high. But this had happened quickly and we weren't at all prepared to suddenly lose Dancer without a fight.

I went to see her on Sunday after church. If a cat's facial expression can beam, Dancer beamed. She immediately stood up and moved toward me, I-V tubes and all, to lick my hand. She purred and purred, as was her style. I got her to eat a little of the kidney diet canned food that was in the small bowl in her cage. I came back the next day and was greeted similarly. Finally on the third day we could take her home. She had revived amazingly.

Confessions of a Cataholic

It wasn't a cure; we were aware of that. There is no cure for feline kidney disease (short of dialysis, which is not a common or reasonable option). But she would have more time with us. We were grateful, and thanked God for this unexpected blessing. Dancer was grateful too, if cats can't be grateful (I think they can).

At home, Dancer refused to eat the kidney diet food the vet prescribed. Who could blame her? It was agreed we would simply let her eat what she wanted to eat. Why starve a cat when she is already ailing? In the meantime I had done some Internet research on feline kidney disease. I discovered that there is controversy about whether the conventional "kidney diet" is a good thing for a sick cat, it being very low in protein when what cats normally eat is virtually all protein and fat. The low protein does reduce phosphorous levels which become too high when the kidneys aren't functioning properly, but it also deprives the cat of nutrients it needs, weakening its muscles.

We ordered a powdered phosphorous binder that can be mixed into canned food, another powder that helps the kidneys metabolize waste, and a special oil full of antioxidants and omega-3 fatty acids contrived by a medical doctor for his own kidney-diseased cat. Those things kept Dancer going well for nearly five months. Every few weeks we would give her a subcutaneous injection of lactated ringers solution to hydrate her, flush out her kidneys and replace electrolytes. She didn't need it more often than that. Those were five precious months.

Then one day about six months after her crisis her kidneys began to shut down again. She stopped eating except for minimal spoonfuls. Every cat has its favorite place in the house to sleep, and that varies with the season, and reasons known only to that cat. When I used my computer in the evening, Dancer had enjoyed lying in the little faux-sheepskin "cathouse" which rested near my right arm on my computer desk. When she could no longer jump up there, she moved to a blanket-lined basket on the living room floor, tucked into an out of the way area near my recliner and Ed's. I could reach my left hand down to pet her as often as I wished, and she loved it. That was no doubt a major reason she chose that spot.

She lay there in the evenings for a number of weeks, but then, as her kidneys again balked, she felt the need to move. She went to our bed and lay on Ed's pillow. Lying on our bed pillows is something the cats know they are not supposed to do, and Dancer was a well-behaved cat. But the pillow was soft (and permeated with Ed's scent) and she was surely becoming more achy and fatigued. She still came to eat with the others for a few days, though she ate very little.

A few days later, a Thursday, she stayed on our bed all day, burrowed under a throw on top of the regular blankets. I became mildly alarmed. I wondered whether her body was shutting down and whether she felt cold. I called the emergency clinic, since they had her kidney disease history. A vet assistant asked if she had a fever or if her temperature was low. I didn't know. After further discussion I hung up and took Dancer's temperature. It was normal. Nevertheless, I got out our heating pad, turned it on low and put it under a towel and Dancer on top of it. She purred. When I went out that afternoon I bought her an oblong fleece bed. She loved that too.

After a few days she was no longer interested in the heating pad. In the meantime I had had to spend a lot of time every day getting her to eat bits of canned food I would puree. And now we gave her subcutaneous injections every evening. I would warm the bag of lactated ringers in a large bowl in the kitchen sink. At first we brought Dancer to the kitchen in her basket bed from the living room. That worked, but after four nights we decided to just bring the paraphernalia to her as she lay on our bed in her fleece bed. All five other cats would gather round to observe the ritual and make sure everything was ok with Dancer.

Occasionally she would let out a little *ouch* sort of meow when the needle went in, but often she didn't make a sound. She knew we were attempting to help, however bizarre the methods may have seemed to her, and she trusted us utterly. But she never got used to the taste of that vile oil we shoved down her throat. She yowled and carried on during that procedure in her best strong voice like she used to when Digory would chase her. And then it would be over, and I'd console her and pet her, and all was instantly forgiven.

From that Thursday to the next I spent a great deal of time caring for Dancer, preparing her food and trying to get her to eat a bit every few hours, giving her medicine, checking on her, reassuring her, petting her. (Since becoming a freelancer I worked out of a home office most of the time, and so was home during the day.)

At night she now stayed in her fleece bed but slept in it wedged between Ed and me. The following Tuesday night Dancer didn't want to stay in that cat bed. She crawled up to me, lay on my chest and put her face under my chin. She purred and purred.

Twice while I was still awake I heard her breath come up short, then a sudden exhale. They were deep sighs, which were both wonderful and ominous; they seemed to indicate utter contentment, sick as she was, but they also sounded to me as if she had momentarily stopped breathing. I prayed then that God would simply allow her to die a quiet peaceful death and that we would not have to make that horrible decision for another beloved cat. I wanted the easy way out for myself (and Ed) as much as for Dancer.

I realized that Dancer would not be with us much longer. I wondered why she had suddenly wanted to be so physically close to me, but I relished the fact that she did. I believe she knew better than we did how ill she was and how short her days would be, with or without our "help." The next night she insisted she wanted to get right at the head of the bed between Ed's pillow and mine, another place she knew she was not supposed to be. After bringing her down and putting her into her fleece bed a few times – she insisting on crawling back up there each time – I left her where she wanted to be.

All that week Ed and I had talked off and on about what was to be done for Dancer. Should we re-hospitalize her? The emergency vet thought that that would give her more time, perhaps as much as three or four months. But at what cost to her? And at what financial cost? We want to be good Christian stewards of whatever resources God sees fit to give us. We questioned whether it would be right (or possible) to spend a thousand or 1500 dollars not to heal a cat but to keep her alive a little longer, no one knew how much longer, and more for our sakes than hers.

What made our decision about her future a nasty one was that, despite her barely eating and her now living on the bed day and night, she simply didn't act like a dying cat. She purred (but of course!), she paid attention when I talked to her and responded with her eyes, her paws and with more purrs. Her eyes, in fact, still looked quite bright. Like Marple, this cat was not about to lie down in a corner and die, though it may well have been time.

On Wednesday, just when it seemed that she had stopped eating for good, she lapped up a particularly copious amount of pureed food, confounding me. On the way back to the kitchen with her food dish I complained to Ed, half-pleased, half-exasperated, "Wouldn't you know! Now she's eating like there's no tomorrow!" Then it occurred to me: "And there isn't!" I blurted out, realizing only after I said it exactly what I was saying. Ed started to laugh and then I laughed to. It was much needed comic relief, if of a rather black kind.

We had made an appointment with our regular vet, Dr. Martin Downey, for that Thursday. Though I told the assistant when I called that Dancer might need to be euthanized, we just weren't sure. We still had some days to think about it when I made the appointment. As that afternoon came, we *still* weren't sure what would be best for Dancer. How horrible it would be to prematurely kill her. We wanted Dr. D.'s advice. We hoped, after hearing his assessment, that we would be able to make the right decision. Of course we knew he couldn't make it for us.

On the way to the clinic Dancer was in her blanket-lined basket which rested on my lap. We also had Cassie with us, in a carrier, because she needed some blood work done. Cassie could see through to the front seat and was docile and quiet. No doubt she sensed something out of the ordinary in Ed's mood and mine, and perhaps in Dancer herself.

I hoisted my knees higher so that Dancer, in her basket, was high enough to look out the window. I suddenly got a flashback of those pleasant days, years earlier, when she was the perfect little passenger on the way to my office. Now, I could see her face in the passenger-door mirror. She looked inquisitive and interested in the world, as ever. I bit my tongue to hold back my tears. Was euthanizing her the answer? I still wasn't sure.

We were led into a different room than the usual cat examining room – a dog room. A large table that doubled as a scale took up much of one end of the room. The unfamiliar surroundings made me uneasy. I almost asked a vet tech if we could move to our regular room, but in the end said nothing. Dr. D. was a few minutes late, and that too made me nervous.

I sat on a bench against one wall with Dancer in her basket on my lap, continually petting her head and back and periodically talking to her. After a serious mysterious illness when she was three years old she always feared going to the vet. In fact, when we were still seeing Dr. Brash, she knew the way so well (informed by that innate global positioning system cats seem to possess) that after several specific turns meant beyond doubt that THE VET was our destination, Dancer would begin to whine and yowl. She never did that in the car otherwise.

Now, smelling the dog smell of the room, and having encountered a couple of particularly loud dogs in the foyer, Dancer was scared. When I took the blanket away from around her I saw that she had deposited a tiny turd on the towel. I took her out of the basket, put her on the stainless steel table, took the turd away with a piece of paper towel and turned a clean portion of her towel to the outside.

Dancer continued her stress-induced bowel movement on the table. When it was clear she was done, I put her back in her basket, sat down with it and petted and talked to her again. She calmed down. But she wasn't relaxed. That pained me but there wasn't more I could do for her. Ed stood next to me, now and then petting Dancer. Ed couldn't sit down; there were no armchairs in the room, a necessity for him, as he needs to brace his own arms on the chair arms in order to be able to hoist himself to a standing position when he wants to get up again.

Dr. D. came in then. Since he hadn't treated Dancer for the kidney disease – we explained about the holiday and follow-up – we filled him in and gave him a copy of Dancer's blood work from earlier that week. He told us that, yes, he could give Dancer an I-V flush again, but would not do it without giving her blood as well. She was seriously anemic. We knew that from the blood tests, but the other vet had apparently not seen a need for a transfusion. That put a somewhat different light on the situation. There is a quick blood test that could be done that would within a few minutes let us know if she was now even more anemic than she was four days earlier. She was; not by a lot, but enough. And she had lost a few more ounces of weight.

We talked more about how we should proceed and gradually we felt the doctor was giving us the knowledge we needed to make a decision. There was no good answer to how long Dancer would live with another round of treatment. We had done very well by her, Dr. D. thought, and were certainly justified in having hospitalized her the first time. He would have done the same, he said. We could also take her home for the weekend, decide what direction we would go, and take that direction on Monday.

That statement suddenly crystalized for me what we needed to do.

Dancer

Caring for Dancer and trying to do what was best for her had been taking its toll on me. I was feeling the stress. I have an auto-immune gastrointestinal illness that does not react well to stress. I just couldn't do it any longer. And Dancer, I knew in my heart of hearts, couldn't really take it any longer herself.

"I think we need to say goodbye to her now," I heard myself say, regretting every word as it came out of my mouth. Ed concurred. We told Dr. D. of the horrific experience we had had with Marple at the end. He assured us that would not happen; a catheter in Dancer's vein would control exactly how much anesthetic she would be given. Dr. D. explained the procedure carefully and kindly. During normal vet visits he was a talkative, good-natured guy, somebody wholly absorbed in fascination with his work and the problems the animals presented him. Now, we were grateful for his low-keyed, compassionate manner, a quiet side of him we hadn't seen.

He took Dancer out to insert the catheter, then brought her back within a few minutes. I asked if I could hold her. "Of course," he said. I took her out of her basket then one last time. Dr. D. suggested I keep the towel under her, in case of a final accident. I held Dancer for a second, then Dr. D. moved in with the syringe.

If one thing could have been different I would have wanted another minute or so to look at and talk to Dancer, to get her face turned toward me. She was looking away from me, perhaps at Ed. Dr. Downey inserted the syringe in the rubber-stopper-like part of the catheter. Almost instantly I felt Dancer's head go slack. I laid her back in the basket. Dr. D. listened for a heartbeat. There was one final breath, a reflex, and Dancer's 16 ½ years had ended. But so had the constant fatigue and discomfort of her final days and weeks.

"Just leave when you wish," Dr. Downey said then, and tucked the blanket around and over Dancer's head. "We'll worry about the bill later. I don't want you to have to stand in line at the desk." And he left the room. Ed and I embraced each other; tears trickled, then poured down my cheeks. I looked at Ed through my tears; his eyes were moist. I lightly stroked Dancer's head with my fingertips. She was warm like always but the wonderfully animating and animated spirit that was Dancer was gone.

I dried my tears as best I could with the Kleenex I had, picked up the basket and Ed opened the door for me. I recall people in the area right outside the door – the dog waiting room was there. I remember wondering if they could see how bad Ed and I felt, or if they could tell I was carrying a dead cat in that basket. Funny what odd, unflinching thoughts arise in difficult moments.

Ed clicked open the automatic door locks of his car, then the trunk. I placed the basket in the trunk then slammed the lid. Right then it seemed peculiar for Dancer to be riding in the trunk. As if she might suffocate.

For the fourth time in our cataholic lives we were experiencing grief over the death of a cat, and for the third time we would bring home a lifeless cat whose housemates would need to know she was no more. I lifted the blanket out of the basket with Dancer in it and gently laid the blanket on the living room rug.

The reactions from those housemates this time, nine long years after Delta's death, struck me as strange. They were quite unlike Delta's reaction to Marple, and Dancer's to both Marple and Delta. The cats were nervous, afraid even. I had to pick each one up, one at a time, and bring it over to Dancer. Caspian was first. I set him down near her. He took a quick look and sniff, shimmied backward away from her, turned and ran. Digory's look and sniff were even faster, and he ran pell-mell away and down the hall. Keeley's reaction was similar to Digory's. Cassie's look and sniff were only slightly less cursory.

Only little Roo, now three years old, stood for a moment to look and sniff, then walked the eight feet or so to the open but screened french doors leading to the deck. She sat down then and began to stare out the door. It had been Roo who had unexpectedly turned into "Nurse Roo" (as Ed would put it) in the last weeks of Dancer's life, and now I could only think that Roo in her catly way was considering what had happened to her friend (and bathtub faucet-drinking mentor).

As Dancer began to spend her week on our bed, which would be the last week of her life, Roo would go and lie down next to her, either in the afternoons or in the evenings. Much of the time Dancer was under a coverlet, but that didn't matter. Roo would sink down beside her and curl up next to the blanket bundle that was Dancer. Sometimes she would stay there for hours.

Previous to Dancer's illness we had noticed Dancer and Roo occasionally touching noses in greeting, something Dancer never did with Digory, Cassie or Keeley, and only occasionally with mild-mannered

Dancer

Caspian. There was communication going on between them – in that last week also – that we knew nothing of. In the next few days it was clear that Roo missed Dancer. What the others felt was less clear, though Digory seemed out of sorts for a few days and Caspian moped some. It was hard to discern any specific reaction from Cassie and Keeley.

That sad Thursday was a day of lovely weather. The ancient gnarled apple tree in our short back yard just off our deck was in profuse bloom. Delicate white blossoms covered the tree, a sweetly scented canopy, though some had already fallen on the bare ground underneath the tree. That would be a fine place to bury Dancer. All the cats spent time, especially in the warm seasons, looking out the full-length windows of the french doors to the deck. From there the apple tree was beautifully visible.

Dancer, especially, loved that spot. In the four years we had lived in our current house, I would often walk by from my home office in the next room to see Dancer, sometimes in proximity to one or more of the other cats, sometimes alone, staring out the doors, watching birds in the apple tree, squirrels scampering, or just enjoying the sun's warmth. Or she would jump up onto the love seat near those doors. It was angled to give a human sitter – or a cat – a pleasant view of the patio plants, tree and slightly beyond.

Ed and I took Dancer's bagged body outside then and dug her grave under the apple tree. We uncovered what would become a foot-high pile of rocks while we dug. At a good depth we placed Dancer in the hole. I snapped off a twig full of apple blossoms, placed it on the bag, then we covered the hole. We topped it with a large rock I had already set aside from my recent pond re-landscaping project, and we added some of the rocks we had just uncovered. A few days later I planted there a burgundy marigold and some ivy, and a little later still I added a clover-leafed plant with dark burgundy tinges mixed with the usual green. The popular name of the plant is Dark Dancer.

On the weekend after Dancer's death, as I was using the date book I keep in my purse I happened to see the entry for Thursday, May 14. It said merely, "Vet. 3:00." An instant lump in my throat almost choked me and tears came again unbidden. That stark entry said nothing of the importance or pain of that day. I added this note, for my own consolation, because I assumed no one else would ever see it: *Dancer died today. R.I.P. little Dancer Cat. What a lovely, loyal cat you were. We will miss you dearly.*

We do miss her dearly. And we will for a long time to come. In the weeks since I've realized just how much, and how long it may take for the grief to dissipate.

I printed a particularly beautiful and characteristic photo of Dancer from my computer and made a card which we sent to Dr. Downey, thanking him for his kindness. What we didn't expect was to get one from him:

> *Please accept my deepest sympathy in the loss of Dancer last week. I know the decision to say goodbye to her didn't come easily and if I could have offered you a better prognosis, I know you would have tried to help her regardless of her age. Without a doubt, it is very apparent that all of your cats are deeply loved and considered members of your family. I know that she is missed, but you should celebrate in the fact that she had such a full and long life, and there is no question much of that is due to being in a wonderful, loving home with people that cared deeply for her....*

Every cataholic should be fortunate enough to have a caring and competent vet. And every cataholic should be blessed with at least one cat like Dancer.

Dancer, lovely as ever, despite the shaved right leg: souvenir of her first bout with kidney disease

4. Digory & Caspian: The Good Buddies

Digory

A month and a half after Marple died in the fall of 1995, Ed and I both began thinking of getting another cat. Delta was then 11 years old; Maple was three; and Dancer still seemed nearly a baby at not yet two. We hadn't talked about a new cat very specifically and so hadn't made plans. We figured that one of these days we'd stop by one of the shelters; or we would acquire a kitten or cat from someone who had one that needed a home.

But one Friday afternoon as I was leaving work, I stopped at the Lincoln County Humane Society in Ontario, just to look around (I told myself). The urge to stop was almost irresistible. Needless to say, I did not resist it. The compulsion wasn't quite as strong as that same kind of urge had been when I had stopped at the Rainbow Shelter and it had resulted in our acquiring Dancer. But it was powerful, nonetheless. And I told myself, "Look how well *that* turned out!"

There were only seven or eight, possibly ten, cats at the LCHS at the time. Peculiarly, most of them were brown tabbies of varying ages, including several kittens as young as 10 or 12 weeks. I've been a sucker for brown tabbies ever since I can remember – long before Marple came into my life and then Ed's as a cherished example of that breed. To me, tabbies have the look of true cats.

The cats of Ed's and my world have good-sized, pointed ears; slightly almond-shaped eyes without tear duct problems; properly protruding inquisitive noses; short, self-groomable, untangled fur; and lithe, relatively long bodies – as opposed to those squat, flat-faced, round-eyed, long-haired creations I think of as the cat equivalent of the yippy-yappy dogs I so dislike. I realize I've probably just alienated some of my readers. I do wish you the joy of such cats if you love them (and all living, breathing cats need to be loved, to be sure; but those kinds of "cats" create no spark of joy in *me*).

I spied a kitten, perhaps 12 weeks old, who clearly would grow up with the catly characteristics Ed and I admire. Every time I walked away from him he came to the front of his cage to try to regain my attention.

His little face was winsome, cute in the best sense of that word. His nose had the simultaneously pointed yet squared features that made him look like a miniature lion, and his white whiskers were inordinately long. His eyes were a pale yellow-green. His coat, even at that young age, was striking. His forehead bore the typical tabby "M" like a side-turned misshapen mark of Zorro. His sides were covered with a combination of black stripes and spots, unique yet not untypical of a tabby. The ticked fur – multicolored, banded hairs – around the stripes and spots seemed to reflect whatever light shone on it, creating another color altogether, a sort of golden glow which in turn highlighted the black spots and stripes, making them appear shiny. Later, when we saw him in sunlight, this effect was startlingly magnified; his coat glistened arrestingly. He would be a beautiful cat.

He was not afraid but was a little shy. Once he understood I would pet him gently and talk to him softly, he purred readily when I was allowed to take him from his cage and hold him. But time was moving on and I needed to get home to make supper, so I reluctantly put him back in the cage. (Our deal was: I cooked, Ed did the dishes, as we had no dishwasher then.) At supper I told Ed about my after-work detour. I put in a pitch for the little tabby. Ed was amenable.

<u>Digory & Caspian</u>

The next morning, Saturday, I had to go back into Canada for a concert rehearsal of the Ontario-based symphony chorus I'm a member of. Ed would drive his own car and make the 20-minute trip too (20 minutes assuming there was no long line of cars at the border waiting to clear Customs). We would stop at the Humane Society so Ed could see the kitten, and if we agreed he was The Next Great One, we would sign the adoption papers and Ed would take him home.

Adopting a cat from Canada cat wasn't an issue. He simply needed a rabies shot in order to be brought into the U.S., and the kitten had had his initial shots. When he was a little older we would bring him to Dr. Brash – still our vet then – to be neutered.

Ed agreed with my assessment: the kitten was a good-looking little creature who appeared to be friendly and smart. What was not to like? (That question would be answered in one particular way as he grew, but as of then, he was the perfect pet.)

So Ed took him home. Later that afternoon when I arrived home we discussed what to name him. Naming a cat, or any pet, is a fascinating procedure. "Procedure" isn't quite the word. For us it's not a studied process. Somehow, based on the cat's look, behavior and apparent characteristics, a name just seems to come, sometimes out of the blue.

Ed and I had been reading C.S. Lewis's *Chronicles of Narnia* together out loud and were enjoying them as adults as much as any child would. Digory is the title character in the chronicle called "The Magician's Nephew." The name Digory kept suggesting itself for our kitten, and so Digory it was.

Soon, as with all of our cats, a nickname would emerge: Digger. That's merely short for Digory but it began to have comical significance, for Digory turned out to be a literal digger. Whenever he didn't like the canned food being served he would begin to methodically paw the floor around his bowl. If the floor had been the ground outside he would have been well on his way to burying the offending blob. He definitely wasn't trying to bury it to save it for later, as some of the big wild cats do. He wanted it *gone*! And then, he would look up at me in his cutest manner and wait for me to get him something he felt was more palatable. It always worked. I couldn't let the poor little cat starve, after all. Digory would commence the same routine whenever he would heave up a hair ball, neatly trying to "dig" around it, not in it. We admired his attempt to be tidy and his expert ability to communicate his displeasure. It usually made us smile. That is, until he was older. By that time he had finely honed his talent for revealing his discontent in another manner, and it would get him into trouble periodically.

After the enforced semi-isolation all new cats had to go through in order to be initiated into the household, Digory settled in well. He played and gamboled, jumped, rolled and chased – chasing Dancer in particular – as kittens do. As the days passed we realized he had a well-ingrained feisty streak, and Persistence could have been his middle name. If he wanted to chase Dancer, he chased Dancer, though eventually her yowling protestations and swats and punches in the face with claws out made him rethink that particular habit, as I've said.

We adopted Digory on December 12, 1995. By that time, Maple's health had been declining, and four weeks later, as little Digory was settling in nicely, three-and-a-half year old Maple was in serious trouble. At the end of the first week of January we brought Maple to the hospital and during the night of the 10th he died. I've described how undemonstrative and self-contained (or perhaps self-absorbed, if cats can contemplate themselves as people are capable of) Maple was and how little we felt we knew him. That helps explain why only eight days later we set off to get a cat to take Maple's place.

This time we revisited the Rainbow Shelter on our own side of the border, Dancer's home before Home. Ed and I went together. After we had gotten Dancer and before Digory arrived, when the subject of cats came up among our friends, Ed would joke that I was no longer allowed to visit any animal shelter unsupervised. It just wasn't safe! It wasn't a matter of "what the cat drug in" but of what cat I dragged in.

So now Ed and I went together. And he was the one who chose our next cat. Or rather, the cat chose him. Of the four handsome male cats we've had, this one is the most striking. He certainly struck Ed that day, both in looks and personality. (I was on the other end of the room, so hadn't yet seen the cat.) He was no longer a kitten but perhaps a year old, supposedly a rural stray, though he was in mighty fine shape for having been an adult-male stray. Nor did he exhibit any of the emotional trauma that strays sometimes do from fending for themselves in the wide world and having less than pleasant encounters with other animals, not to

66

mention people. We suspected that someone had dumped him in the country but that he had been found and brought to the shelter very quickly.

His feet, legs, belly, chin, lower face and nape of the neck were white, and so were his whiskers. Over his back there appeared to have been thrown a tabby blanket of primarily brown and black. The "blanket" had landed neatly across his back and down his tail, and it hung over his sides. It covered the top of his head and part of the tops of his ears and cheeks. His nose, inner ears and toe pads were pink. His eyes were large and a bright golden yellow. He was the type of cat that immediately elicits the exclamation, "Isn't he beautiful!"

(Prince) Caspian

He immediately came to the front of his cage when Ed approached. The cat rubbed against the cage, trying to get as close to Ed as possible. He sat down then, and patiently waited for something to happen: to be taken out of the cage? to be petted by a hand thrust into the cage? for nothing in particular? He seemed a patient cat, mild-mannered, friendly in an almost self-effacing way.

I, meanwhile, had been peering at a lithe black female with bits of white on her face. The note on her cage said that she would do best in a one-cat household. We were told that her owner, a woman who lived alone, had sorrowfully given up the cat when circumstances forced her to move to an animal-free apartment. But she visited the cat and called every day since she had given it up. I could appreciate the owner's tenacity and could empathize deeply with what must have been her broken heart. But I couldn't imagine giving up Delta, Dancer or Digory.

When I petted the cat and observed her I could tell within a minute – and so could Ed – that *this* was a prima donna, a feline version of She Who Must Be Obeyed. I felt sorry for the poor animal having been

67

separated from her long time owner (and I couldn't help feeling a little judgmental toward a woman who would give up a cat in exchange for an apartment. *Surely there were other places to live that would allow just one cat!* I thought). But I also knew that this was not the cat for us. Delta would have ignored her or put her in her place when necessary. Dancer, too, would have shown her very quickly that she would *not* be the boss; and when that was accomplished Digory would mercilessly tease and chase her, reinforcing the lesson.

Ed had already assessed and dismissed as a possibility for us that hapless black cat (to this day we've never had a black cat and I doubt we ever will). He had moved on to the tabby-and-white across the room, and every time he tried to move away the cat moved toward him, rubbing the cage bars and emitting a soft, squeaky, almost kittenish meow, and the smallest hint of a purr. The cat liked Ed and wasn't going to let him leave if he could help it.

Ed took him out of the cage. For a large cat he was cuddly and clearly enjoyed being held. He wasn't the least bit aggressive. He showed his desire to be gotten out of there by settling into Ed's arms and purring softly. Who could argue that he wasn't a striking animal and obviously good-natured? When Ed put him back in the cage so we could discuss what to do the cat looked forlorn. His golden eyes were as expressive as any cat we knew, and cats' eyes are particularly expressive. He was choosing us; we had no choice but to concur.

Not that we didn't want to. It was easy to picture this easygoing fellow at home with Delta, Dancer and Digory; he might even be a calming influence on rambunctious Digory. We went through the adoption procedure, picked up our free food samples and headed to the car. On the way home we discussed names. We agreed right away to consider another Narnian character as a name source, and we hit on the right one almost immediately. This cat seemed simultaneously mild-mannered and strong. He was sweet-tempered but we doubted he'd be a push-over when it came to the other cats. And though of apparently humble birth, whether back-alley or born in a barn, he was as beautiful as any pedigreed cat could be. He was a prince of a cat; he would be Prince Caspian.

When we got home we began our introduce-a-new-cat routine once more. We put Caspian in the guest room. We brought in a litter box, put down plastic on the floor under it and let Caspian out of the carrier. Little Digory was instantly intrigued with the smell of the newcomer. So was Dancer, which surprised me a little, as she could be reticent with human strangers and the more so with other animals. Delta, too, eventually came around to check him out. Digory camped out in the hallway, lying at the base of the door, with Caspian on the other side doing the same. Within a day we could put Caspian in the carrier, open the room door and let the others in to check him out, and he them.

There was no hissing from any of the cats, nor other indications from any of them that said, "Back off!" So we could very quickly let Caspian out of the carrier and allow the others into the room one at a time – supervised by me. That went well. Caspian was already one of the family.

Digory and Caspian became good buddies and soon were sleeping together and grooming each other. Digory readily acknowledged Caspian's dominance even though the latter was the newcomer. Digory was only four or five months old then, still really a kitten, while Caspian was about a year old. Delta and Caspian treated each other with respect. Dancer and Caspian were also fine together and clearly respected each other too, though they, like Delta and Caspian, never became intimate buddies. Being a spayed female and a neutered male and relatively close in age, Dancer and Caspian seemed to relate to each other as equals, though Dancer never allowed Caspian to groom her (and nor did Delta).

With each day it became more apparent that Caspian had as handsome a personality as he did physical appearance. There grew a special bond between Ed and Caspian. Caspian clearly liked me all right (I fed him, after all, and oh how he loved his food!). But he particularly warmed up to Ed and would crawl up onto Ed's recliner with him and sit at Ed's feet or on his shins for most of an evening. Digory would sometimes join him, but generally Digory loved my lap. Digory would lie on my upper legs while Dancer would curl near my feet. Delta, while still with us, generally snoozed upstairs.

When a friend of ours asked me about our new cat and I began to describe Caspian, after naming his physical characteristics I found myself calling him things like mild-mannered, sweet-tempered, strong, knowing what he likes but not the kind of cat to get in your face or be aggressive. It suddenly struck me that Ed and Caspian are rather alike. I told our friend, "Picture Ed as a cat. Or: picture a cat with a likeable personality like Ed's!" She laughed and knew exactly what I meant. Ed rolled his eyes and made noises aimed at me that meant, "Pain in the tush!" But I think he secretly enjoyed what I said. It's been a standing joke in the well over a decade since.

Not long after Caspian came home to us he demonstrated that he could be a mighty hunter. No, we didn't let him outside loose, though we had already introduced him to a halter and leash, which he adapted to immediately and loved. He became, instead, the Sock Prowler and the Dishcloth Demon.

As I've described, our bedroom in our Lewiston house, where we still lived, was upstairs. The cats had the run of the house from attic to basement, including the laundry room, which had no door. One night somewhat after midnight we were awakened by loud, insistent cat calls of the type that any cat owner recognizes as hunting cries meaning, "I've got something! I've got something! It's alive! Look!" And so Caspian would drag his prey up the two flights of stairs from the basement to deposit it on or near our bed with a final satisfied chirp.

His kills were socks, one at a time; a dish towel or dish cloth, a hand towel, a T-shirt now and then; and once or twice even a bath towel. Over the years he accumulated an impressive number of trophies. We don't know the exact number that resulted from his almost nightly toil, but we figured that the T-shirts and bath towels qualified as big game. We washed and recycled his prey, unbeknownst to him.

Somehow he pilfered all these from the laundry hamper. I say somehow because the laundry hamper is at least three feet high, a foldable, soft-sided bag of vinyl-covered cloth on a frame. It's sturdy enough – we're still using it nearly 14 years later – but not something a large 12-pound cat could perch on the edge of in order to go fishing for its contents. He must have catapulted from the floor into the depths of the hamper, grabbed what he wanted, then jumped out again. Occasionally he wouldn't bother to go down to the basement. He would simply head for the kitchen and steal a drying dish towel that had been stretched out along the stove handle.

As I write, Caspian is now past 14 ½ and we moved to our current house when he was 10. But he still goes on night time reconnaissance after all these years. Now he does it in spurts, night after night, then will suddenly stop for a while. And he no longer bothers to snatch socks from the laundry hamper. He can't jump as high as he used to;

but he has also become a bit lazy (he's entitled at his relatively mature age). Annoyingly, his prey has become exclusively dish towels and table placemats, often clean ones just put out. They're easy to capture.

One winter night in his early years Caspian got his chance to encounter real prey, though prey is not quite the word, as not a drop of blood was shed, no necks were snapped, no tendons severed.

It was an exceptionally cold winter in the Niagara region. The area is a fruit and vineyard belt – climate Zone 6 for you gardeners. The temperatures are normally mitigated by the region being a peninsula sandwiched between two of the Great Lakes, Ontario and Erie. But day after day it was barely above 10 degrees Fahrenheit, and at night it would drop to zero and frequently below. Previous to the cold snap it had snowed heavily. When it stopped I dug a path from our patio out to the bird feeder at the back of the yard feeling like I was on the way to being Moses and the children of Israel crossing the Red Sea. The snow topped two-and-a-half feet and the walls lining my path gradually grew twice that high.

During the day our bird feeder was a busy place. Even a red-tailed hawk dropped by once (instantly scattering all the other avian diners). But at night the buffet was empty. On this night there was an exception of one species: the opossum. 'Possums are foul-smelling, slow-moving, uniquely ugly creatures. They have long, pointed snouts, rat-like prehensile tails, curved, hand-like claws and dead-gray, coarse hair over leathery gray skin. They are scavengers and thus will eat nearly anything, the more so when plant matter or grubs aren't available because of snow, and other possible snacks are safe underground or otherwise hidden away. We knew there were a few opossums living under the shrubbery on the golf course near our shed. The shed was at the end of the flag pole-shaped extension of our yard, abutting golf course property. We had seen the critters occasionally in the fall. But now one fellow, made bold by hunger, came out to see what we had to offer.

First he snorkeled up all the ground-lying seed the birds had overlooked. Then he waddled his way up my path (as if I had done all that work just for him), clambered onto the patio and headed straight for the two recycling bins that stood just outside our back door in winter. One of those bins contained empty cat can food cans. Though I always rinsed them out before chucking them into the proper bin, clearly they still held an enticing aroma for the 'possum.

He began loudly rummaging around in the bin, turning over and inspecting can after can. The noise alerted us to an intruder. I turned on the back light, which startled him. He turned and fled back up the path as fast as his stubby legs could carry him. Caspian had heard the commotion before I turned the light on, as had Digory and Dancer. But Caspian, unlike the other two, boldly ran up to the door and eagerly peered out (it had a full-length window). When the light snapped on, laid-back Caspian got as charged up as we had ever yet seen him. He chirped and yelped and meowed excitedly. Digory and Dancer were also acutely interested but were much more cautious and stayed back a ways from the door.

I wasn't keen on the opossum getting used to rifling our recycling bins. I knew Caspian wouldn't attack an adult opossum so I opened the door for him. He bounded out. I was curious to see what he would do. I was hoping he would scare the 'possum just enough to prevent it from coming right up to the house again. I expected our brave feline to hiss, perhaps, and stand guard on the patio while the 'possum receded down the path into the night.

But Caspian went one much better than that. Wholly untypical of him, he charged after the 'possum, which was as yet only about halfway down the path to the bird feeder and the back of the yard.

When the 'possum sensed (surely smelled) Caspian, he urged his short legs to hit top speed. But of course there was no way he could outrun a cat. Within a few seconds Caspian was on the 'possum's tail. Not quite literally on it, but within striking distance, had he wanted to strike. But Caspian is a wimp at heart. (Disclaimer: in saying that, and having likened Caspian to Ed, I'm not implying that wimpiness is one of Ed's characteristics.)

Caspian suddenly stopped, then backed up a little as the 'possum continued to hurry forward. Our poor cat simply didn't know what to do. He was perplexed. The 'possum was about his size but had much longer, sharper teeth and claws. Caspian wasn't so stupid as to attack such a creature, as I knew he wouldn't be. Yet as we've seen in various scenarios in the dozen years since, despite his normally easy-going nature he has a knack for charging ahead when he gets excited, and *then* engaging his little cat brain to figure out whether that was actually the right thing to do.

Where most cats (and our other cats) would be cautious and tread carefully before jumping into an unknown situation, Caspian may barrel in (his occasional timidity notwithstanding), then become startled when he finds himself in a position he really didn't want be in and isn't sure how to get out of.

I had quickly thrown a coat on and now stood on the patio watching this unfolding drama. The 'possum headed down the flag-pole-shaped stretch of our yard back to his normal territory as I called Caspian to come back. Caspian moved ahead instead, stopping under the bird feeder, tail nervously twitching, twitching, and still clearly eager to get another glimpse of that odd, smelly creature. (If *we* think 'possums are smelly, imagine how strong they smell to cats.) He knew he had been defeated, however. He turned and came to me then. He was cold by now. I picked him up and carried him back to the house. When we got inside, Dancer and Digory circled and sniffed and sniffed some more while Caspian communicated to them in some way cats do his thrilling but short-lived adventure. Even Delta was there to get in on the story.

Caspian did his job effectively. We had several more very cold nights but the 'possum never trod that path again, and was even cautious about picking up the leftover seeds at the bird feeder.

When spring arrived, the cats were eager for me to fit them into their halters and leashes so they could enjoy the sun's warmth and watch the birds, squirrels and chipmunks. Delta, too, was eager to be outside. When outside, she had long since gotten used to being confined by halter and leash. She lived quite happily, though in partial self-imposed seclusion, for almost five years after Caspian arrived, and always reacted benignly to him. If there is a cat that has had a calming effect on others, whether feline and human, it is Caspian.

On one such lovely spring day a chipmunk unexpectedly met a sad end, much to my surprise. I was not outside with the cats that day, but checked on them regularly to make sure they hadn't gotten their leashes tangled or hadn't gotten into something that might cause injury to any of them.

The third or fourth time I came out to check, Digory ignored me. He was crouched down in the grass staring intently at something a foot or so in front of him. I knew that position and was apprehensive seeing him crouch in that way. I ran over to see what was going on. There was a chipmunk, also lying in the grass, on its side, dead. It had unknowingly come within the range of Digory's leash. Digory happened to be attached to the clothesline lead that day, so of the four cats he had the greatest range to roam. I hadn't seen it happen, but clearly the chipmunk had run into his path and Digory had instinctively pounced. I couldn't very well blame him. It was indirectly my fault. I had seen chipmunks scamper around near the ash tree at one end of the clothes line. Fortunately, it was the one and only death (besides occasional spiders, flies and centipedes) that Digory the hunter ever caused. From then on I kept him on one of the shorter, non-sliding leashes when he and the other cats were out enjoying the yard.

By the time we moved into our current house in March of 2005 Delta had been gone five years, Caspian and Digory had been long-time intimate friends, Dancer was slowing down slightly but thriving, and we had two additional cats: Cassie and Keeley. The five cats naturally needed time to adjust to their new surroundings. Our house occupies one floor (plus a basement) and so is far more spread out horizontally than our previous Cape-Cod-style house was.

The house is on a corner; the front yard is large and tree-filled. But the back yard is far smaller and thus more intimate than our previous back yard was. We decided from Day 1 that in this house the basement door, just off the kitchen, would always remain closed to the cats. There is a partially finished basement under about half of the 40-year-old house, and under the other half is a crawl space which can't be closed off from the rest of the basement and whose floor is dirt – just the kind of remote, dusty place a gaggle of cats would love to hang out in or run to if they didn't want to be caught. And the kind of space from which, indeed, neither Ed nor I would be easily able to retrieve them if that were necessary.

We would not need the basement for the litter boxes as there is a remote half-bathroom at the end of the laundry room hallway. Both that bathroom and the laundry room share their interior wall with the front wall of the garage and are accessed by an L-shaped hallway that leads from the kitchen. We determined immediately that this was a bathroom we would rarely need to use, as there are two others, and it has enough floor space for four side-by-side litter boxes, the fifth one being just outside the bathroom door under the laundry tub. Within five minutes all the cats learned where their boxes were now located. That space has ever since been referred to as the Cat Bathroom.

The cats enjoyed exploring the new rooms and unfamiliar smells. And the familiar scents of all the furnishings they already knew made the adjustment quite easy.

After several weeks in our new house I found the cat leashes and halters, untangled them and set them up in our much smaller (though entirely fenced) back yard. The cats loved being outside again, as always, the more so since everything they saw and smelled was new.

I did not love it. With five cats, each on a 12-or-so-foot leash, needing enough room to avoid entanglement with any of the others, there was little room to maneuver. I was already in the midst of digging a small 10 by 8 pond, putting in three raised beds for vegetables, creating a flower bed along part of the back fence, planting three junipers and some other shrubs around one side of the house, and setting up several bird feeders. In addition, there is a large deck that angles around the back of the house, roughly 15 feet deep and almost 30 feet long. It is close enough to the ground that it requires only one step down to get to the grass or sidewalk. And it can be crawled under if you're an animal the size of a cat or smaller.

That is promptly what Caspian did on his first trip out. When he got to the end of his leash it stopped him, of course, and there he sat, under the deck and out of my reach. Calling and coaxing did nothing. Finally I tugged on the leash hard enough to drag him back near the deck's outer edge. But he had gotten under it by scrunching down, flattening his rather large body to the ground, then shimmying forward. I couldn't exactly explain to him that he would have to do that again in order for me to pull him out, or for him to get himself out. Eventually he did figure it out, and guided by my tugs on his leash he emerged into the grass again, wearing cobwebs and dust but otherwise none the worse for the wear.

After two outdoor leash-and-halter forays at the new house I decided we would call that particular activity quits. I had to watch each wandering cat virtually every minute. I felt like their baby sitter, or more accurately, their nanny. But as the famous commercial suggests, it's tough to herd cats. And once the new plants, including those around the pond, became established, I didn't want them being trampled on, laid on, eaten or otherwise uprooted by merrily oblivious felines.

Soon after we moved, and after I had decided to keep the cats in from then on, Digory shot out the deck door one afternoon as I opened it. He would go looking for his own adventure if I wouldn't provide it. After all these years of living with multiple cats Ed and I are programmed to look around inside before opening any exterior door to make sure no cat is priming for a quick exit. Whether I forgot to do that or just didn't see Digory I don't recall, but such fast escapes still do happen once in a while.

I wasn't worried. Digory was now used to the house and the yard and I was sure – or almost sure – he wouldn't actually run away. If he disappeared for a while, I imagined he would come back before long.

I didn't see what direction he headed. I continued to work in the yard as I had planned to do, periodically calling for Digory as I worked. No response. A couple of hours passed. Then another hour. He still hadn't returned and now I was starting to worry. He was familiar with our yard but not the general area. We live a couple of hundred yards from the road that travels along the U.S. side of the Niagara River. The speed limit is 45 mph, but as on our old road, many people drive faster. On the river side of the road, the bank carries heavy vegetation and drops sharply down to the water.

I described Digory to our next door neighbor, who we had already gotten to know, then set out on my bike to look for our recalcitrant cat. I rode and looked and called. Nothing. Then I set out on foot. Nothing. Ed arrived home and he looked too.

I hopped on my bike one more time, turning north out of our street to go up the road along the river. I had a strong hunch Digory would not have headed in that direction but looked there anyway. He would have had to cross our street first, which he probably wouldn't have done. Going in the other direction he could have slipped through the fence at the back of our yard and headed across various other back yards where there would be plenty to occupy him. I had walked at the back edge of two of those yards previously but he wasn't there. Or he was hidden.

Then I headed south along the river and rode about half a mile. Still nothing. I was upset now. What could have happened to him? Where could he be? He was not yet wearing a tag with our new address and phone number on it, and the numbers listed on the old tag he still wore were no longer working. I turned back toward home riding slowly, trying to scrutinize every bit of each front yard I passed.

Digory & Caspian

The handful of houses in that area are large and several are set back from the road, with expansive front yards. Suddenly I saw a black and white cat in such a yard about 40 feet in front of an impressive two-story white house with a large veranda.

I stopped and stood next to my bike. I looked again. The black-and-white was sitting meat-loaf style, facing me and the road. Less than 20 feet from him was Digory, also sitting on his haunches, facing the other cat. I seemed to have stumbled upon Showdown at the OK Cat Corral. The black-and-white was at home; Digory was intruding on its territory. But they were so close to each other that Digory couldn't take a chance of turning tail and running. The other cat would no doubt catch him in an instant if it wanted to. (I couldn't tell whether it was male or female but I assumed it was another male.)

I put my bike on its kickstand and walked toward Digory. The other cat eyed me but didn't move. I called to Digory, not too loudly. His ears swiveled back. He knew I was there. And in the next instant I knew he was very happy to know it. With me there he could dare to make his getaway. I called him once more. He shot toward me and stopped at my feet. I grabbed him into my arms and looked to see what the other cat was doing. It watched me and Digory for a moment then trotted toward its house. Digory was no longer interested in the cat. I could feel his little heart pounding. I stroked him and told him in a sweet voice what a stupid little feline twit he was and that he had better never do that again. It was a mutual admiration society.

I called Ed on my cell phone to say I'd found the Recalcitrant and wondered whether he should drive there to bring Digory home. I was only four houses around the corner from home but I wasn't sure I could ride while holding Digory in one arm. But Digory was now content to nestle against my chest with his head over my shoulder. I could manage riding a few blocks like that, steering with one hand. When we got back to our house, Digory obviously told his story to Caspian, Dancer, Cassie and Keeley. They gathered round to hear the tale just as he, Delta and Dancer had when Caspian had had his adventure with the opossum.

Digory is a lap sitter *par excellence*. He, above all the other cats, seeks out my lap whenever it is available. When we're still at the dining table, if I've pulled back from the table and am sitting with my legs crossed, he'll hop up and stretch himself out along my upper leg, face toward the table, as Dancer used to do at my office. Then he will wait for me to pet him, which of course I automatically do. If I sit in a recliner after dinner or stretch on the couch or the love seat, up will come Digory to the warmth and comfort of my lap. Sometimes he curls up but usually he's a stretcher, preferring to wedge the length of his body along the length of either my upper or lower legs – usually upper so that he's also within reach of a petting hand. He's no dummy.

Caspian will frequently join Digory, but Digory usually needs to take the lead in this particular department. Occasionally Dancer would come up as well, but would allow some space between herself and the other cats.

As Caspian became a loved addition to the feline family and Dancer became more and more self-assured, Digory began to develop what can only be called a case of jealousy that would become acute once we had several additional cats. It escalated into a serious problem; he began to show his displeasure by peeing in places other than the litter box.

Frequently he and Caspian would have mock fights, and still do, sparring with each other for both entertainment and exercise. It was one of the games they began to play together early on. Only once in a while would it get a little too serious and become what sounded and looked like a real cat fight. That almost never happens now. They both seem to have learned the other's limits, and their own. But when Digory and Dancer would get in each other's hair, as they did now and then, it was serious from the first moment. Claws came out, though they never bit or truly hurt each other.

Digory's jealousy emerged after he noticed that Dancer was getting attention from me when he wasn't; and it annoyed him. My giving attention to Caspian didn't bother him, however. Digory still deferred to Caspian as the dominant cat. But he saw Dancer as an equal, or perhaps as subordinate to himself.

The first time I discovered that Digory had peed outside the litter box after such an incident I surmised that since he didn't dare lash out at me for providing the attention that irked him, he took out his frustration on Dancer by lashing out at her, and then indirectly on me by doing something he absolutely knew he shouldn't do, something that was sure to get my and Ed's attention.

We've trained our cats in the finer points of the House Rules for

Felines through verbal commands initially accompanied (and periodically still accompanied) by quick squirts from a water bottle. There are essentially three things they may not do: climb onto or sit on the dining room table, kitchen island and counters; paw or claw the screen doors; and claw the upholstered or leather furniture. They all understand, and now, a strong "No!" and the suggestion of being hit with a stream from the squirt gun keeps them on the straight and narrow most of the time – except Digory.

For all of the nearly 20 years since Ed and I began our life together with just Marple and Delta, we've been careful to try to give each of our cats the care and attention he or she needs. Every feline personality has its quirks, likes, dislikes and specific characteristics. When you spend a lot of time with your cats it's easy to observe what each one enjoys in attention, affection, types of food, toys and games.

Nevertheless, Digory has continued to act out like a problem child when he feels slighted, or sometimes after I yell at him for pawing the deck door screen, for snapping with a front paw the wooden grilles on the other door to the deck, or trying to hone his claws on the leather of my recliner. The other cats simply don't do those things (though Roo has picked up a milder version of the screen and leather fetish from Digory).

The others always respond quickly to verbal reprimands in the rare event they try to do something they've been taught not to do. Digory responds to the water bottle (mostly), but then later I may find a little puddle of urine on the kitchen or bathroom floor. Twice he has done that on my music-book bag (waterproof and washable, fortunately) and once actually on one of the kitchen counters.

These instances have occurred only occasionally, over months, even years; it has not happened often. Nevertheless, it's a pattern, and it's related to his ultra-sensitivity to my disapproval or his jealousy of one of the other cats, usually Roo or Keeley. The irony, of course, is that peeing on the floors or a book bag is not guaranteed to win a cat his owner's approval. And so such a cycle becomes vicious if it is not systematically worked at to correct.

All that said, Digory isn't a bad cat. Neurotic, maybe, but not bad! The more I've consciously tried to assure him that he is as much loved as his feline family members are, through petting, holding him and talking to him, the better he responds, naturally. In that way animals are much like people. That approach is helping. His bad episodes now happen only sporadically, but have not been entirely eliminated.

Digory may possibly be a "work in progress" for the rest of his life. Nevertheless, he's a smart, interesting cat who is capable of great affection. His almost nightly lap sitting is an especially sweet quality, something I enjoy as well as he obviously does. And when I am feeling low he shows particular interest in me. Then he reveals some of the "Nurse Farfel" quality that Marple was famous for.

When Dancer was ill with her kidney disease, though she was his nemesis for many years, he showed unexpected solicitousness toward her. Digory was among the first to be there when the feline clan would gather round each night as Ed and I prepared to give Dancer her subcutaneous injections during her last few weeks. And when she would yowl in protest at the nasty-tasting oil we poured down her throat, Digory would come running, a look of concern on his face. Digory not only looks somewhat like Marple did but has many of the same good traits she had. That's a very a fine thing to be said of any cat.

Digory is about six months younger than Caspian, and Caspian turned 14 in January of 2009. While Digory still annoyingly paws the screen-door frame and snaps the door grille once the weather warms up and he wants to join us outside, he is mellowing. When Dancer had been missing from our lives for barely a month, I already detected a subtle change in Digory and a shift in relationship between several of the cats. While Roo had taken on the Nurse Farfel role with Dancer, the development of that closer relationship had actually started somewhat earlier, initiated by Dancer, who began to get friendlier with Roo. But now that Dancer is gone, Digory and Roo seem to be gradually gravitating toward each other, or are at least friendlier. That's a good sign, since Digory had previously seen Roo as an object of jealousy.

Caspian started out as mellow as they come but has become even more laid back, which I didn't think possible. He is more affectionate than he was in his early years and now purrs both readily and loudly. He also seeks out attention and affection when he wants it instead of waiting for it to come to him, or hoping it does. He often comes to me as I'm working at my computer and emits his friendly little yelp that means, "I'd like you to pick me up, please." He's always polite about it. He doesn't whine or insist. So of course I do pick him up and cram him head first into the fleece "cathouse" near my right arm that Dancer used to sleep in. I say "cram" because he's considerably bigger than Dancer was and can barely wedge himself in. But that seems to be why he loves it. The smaller the bed or bag or box he can stuff his big body into, the better he likes it. Caspian is a lovable and lovely cat by any standard.

Life is best for Caspian and Digory when they are lying a few feet from Ed or me. That's why they have both decided (now that Dancer and Cassie are gone) that sleeping on our bed wedged on or between Ed and me is a pretty fine place to spend the night, and an even better place every morning, when a human hand is likely to reach out and offer a petting, for 10 minutes at a stretch.

Digory & Caspian: perfect posers

5. Cassie: The Medical Miracle

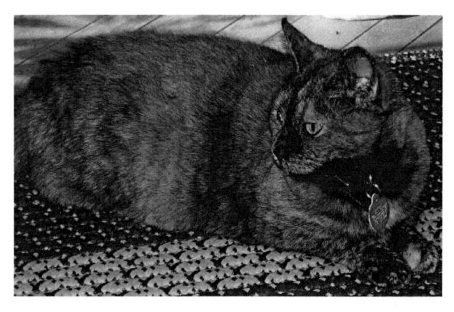

Cassie

For one year and eight months in the mid-1990s Ed and I lived with four cats: Delta, Dancer, Digory and Caspian. Then one Saturday morning in August of 1997 I went out to a shelter unsupervised again. Well, it wasn't exactly a shelter. It was an adopt-a-thon sponsored by a pet adoption organization. Save-a-Pet held the event at one of the major pet food and supply stores in the area.

I hadn't gone there to look at the cats up for adoption. I had gone to buy cat food. But a dozen cats in cages were hard to miss. They were just inside the large main entrance. I don't recall what any of the cats looked like except the one that we adopted in the end. I do recall there being no kittens there; the animals were all young cats or mature adults who desperately needed homes.

Save-a-Pet refuses to euthanize healthy animals. It puts the animals it receives into foster homes until it can find permanent homes for them. Periodically it gets a boost in finding those homes by holding adopt-a-thons at prominent pet supply stores. It also puts ads in local papers so that would-be adopters can directly contact a cat's foster caregiver. And it o holds auctions and various other events to raise money to help care for the fostered animals.

The cat I was drawn to was, like Caspian when we got him, about a year old. She had had kittens a couple of months earlier and they had recently been adopted. Now, she too, very much needed a home.

She was a small cat. A tortoiseshell, she was full of the colors that I most like in a cat: rust, brown, tan, cream, black and various shades of all of those. She had a striking, perfectly straight line down her chin and throat. Harlequin-like, on one side of the line the fur was entirely black, on the other side the fur was the multicolor typical of tortoiseshells. A black line also ran down the middle of her head and spread to cover part of each ear. All four of her paws were primarily black.

She was excessively friendly and meowed for attention when I turned from her. (That should have told me something about her but I didn't pick up on it at the time.) She reveled in being petted and had a loud and constant purr. She purred even when I put her back in her cage and when I simply stood and watched her. Those were points in her favor, I decided, and I was certainly right about that. None of our other cats except Dancer has been such an indiscriminate purrer.

The cat had already been named Cassie by her foster caregiver. Cassie had been in that home throughout most of her pregnancy and until her kittens were weaned, about four months. Though "Cassie" was not a name Ed or I would have chosen had she not already been named, we decided to keep it. It somehow fit her, I can't explain exactly why.

If Cassie purred readily she also whined indiscriminately, we soon found out. That trait shocked us; we had never before encountered it in a cat. It seemed to be the equivalent of a dog being a constant barker, which nobody likes, but which can be cured with proper training. Not so with a cat. Or at least, we never found a way to alleviate it, though it cured itself for a while.

After we had her for a month or so, Cassie began sitting next to, or on, me or Ed when we were reading or watching TV in the living room. She would purr loudly and long, for many minutes at a time. She seemed content and was demonstrating that all was right with her world, we concluded. She was the perfect cat – for that month as she adjusted to her new home and housemates, feline and human. That adjustment made, when she wanted to eat, she whined; when she wanted attention, she whined; when Delta, Digory, Caspian or Dancer did something that displeased her, she whined.

"Whine" is the only word for her kind of vocalizing. This was not a meow of any sort. As my fellow cataholics know, every cat's voice is different and each cat has a repertoire of unique meows and other sounds. Each signifies something specific to the cat and its buddies – if not always to the human beings listening; some are hard to interpret.

But this was different. This was *whining,* pure and simple: a loud, insistent, nasal-sounding, irritating utterance repeated over and over and over; the kind of noise – *noise* – that is hard to tune out and that, as a result, gets on your nerves. It's a cat's means of yelling or complaining; or at any rate, it was Cassie's means. It was the kind of cacophony that you might hear in a bad dream, making you want to strangle the little bugger emitting such unmusical, incessant wrawling.

Of course I wouldn't hurt our cats or any cat in any way for any reason. But when Cassie got into a whining mood – which was at least a couple of times a day, every day, seven days a week, month after month, year after year, it made one push the envelope of evil thoughts about doing her damage.

Except when she was hungry or was clearly annoyed by one of her feline buddies, we could determine no good reasons why she should whine so. She seemed to have emotional problems. Perhaps I exacerbated those problems by withdrawing from her somewhat because of that constant complaining. It began to be hard to truly love a cat that whines all the time. I became aware that I wasn't seeking her out to lavish attention on her as I did the others. Ed involuntarily had the same reaction. But we just couldn't help it. Her whining drove us nuts. She, in turn, became increasingly pushy, both in noisily demanding attention, affection or food – and in dealing with her fellow cats.

Interestingly (and quite amazingly to us), that whining and pushiness didn't seem to bother them. Delta was still with us for about two-and-a-half years after Cassie arrived; she simply steered clear of the loud-mouth. Dancer did the same, and Cassie was smart enough not to make demands on either of her fellow females. Digory, however, would happily share our bed or any cat bed, blanket or towel with Cassie, and often he, Cassie and Caspian would curl up as a threesome. Cassie having had a short career as a mother may have played a role. She was motherly with her male buddies, grooming them often, on their heads and throats, particularly.

They returned the favor, though she usually initiated it. Their favorite past time whenever Cassie came into their vicinity was to greet her by sniffing her butt. And not just a quick sniff. Digory particularly relished this activity and he could often be seen afterward with his mouth open and upper lip curled up, putting into action his Jacobson's (vomeronasal) organ, a cat's pheromone detector. It enables the cat to get the best possible whiff of whatever it wants or needs to smell. No other female cat of the six we've had was so irresistibly attractive in that manner to the males of the species. Though all the cats had been spayed or neutered, Cassie was obviously emitting a strong scent, and a wildly attractive one as far as Digory and Caspian were concerned. When Keeley entered the household, he, too, began to find Cassie's backside utterly compelling.

In 2007, when Cassie was 11 years old, there began a saga which drastically altered her life and therefore changed ours too. She began to lose weight. She was eating more than ever and was demanding food even more often than she ever had before, yet she was becoming thinner and thinner. She acted hyperactive, interspersed with long periods of the sleep of the near-dead. This behavior seemed to come on quickly.

The previous year we had begun seeing our new vet, Martin Downey, a Canadian married to an American. He lived in the U.S. and had just opened his own clinic in western New York. It was a nicely designed facility and we had found Dr. Downey to be a knowledgeable, enthusiastic and outgoing practitioner of the veterinary art. A sign in the lobby of the clinic says, "All God creatures welcome here," but like most small-animal clinics, mostly dogs and cats passed through the doors.

We brought Cassie in at the appointed time for an exam and explained her symptoms. Dr. D. very quickly suggested she might have a hyperactive thyroid, a condition that, unknown to us at the time, is becoming increasingly common in cats. (One theory suggests that the chemical fire retardants in upholstery, rugs and bedding, which cats lick off their fur after having lain on upholstery, rugs or bedding, could be a cause.) A blood test would verify whether our vet's hunch about the hyperthyroidism was correct.

It was. Our choices to have it treated were radioactive iodine (which was an actual cure but which was frightfully expensive, needing to be done at a facility that treats people); surgery; or daily medication – methimazole, also developed for people, not animals. We opted for the pills. The medicine would take effect quickly but in a few months Cassie's blood would need to be rechecked to make sure the dose she was being given was still correct.

Cassie's behavior normalized, so did her appetite and so did her weight. Her next blood work was fine. She went back to being her old simultaneously purry-whiny self. But with the next check after that we learned that she would need a bit more methimizole, now morning and evening instead of once a day. Her condition again normalized, though now instead of being hyperactive Cassie became somewhat lethargic.

Happily, some months passed without incident. Then I began to notice that Cassie seemed to be sleeping more. Whether a cat actually *is* sleeping more can be hard to tell since they are naturally the champion sleepers of the world.

One Sunday morning as I was in the kitchen and the cats waited for their breakfast Cassie seemed disoriented. She was clearly hungry but didn't go over to her bowl when I set it down in its place (each cat has his or her own bowl and spot to eat). Cassie was facing in the wrong direction and didn't appear to know where her bowl was. That seemed rather odd, but I dismissed the thought at the time. I turned her around and placed her in front of her bowl. We were about to leave for church, and as I'm the organist and choir director and had to be there early, I had no leisure time to think about any possible implications of Cassie's newly strange behavior.

When we returned home nothing seemed out of the ordinary. The cats greeted us, slept, watched the birds and squirrels, slept – their normal Sunday afternoon. Cassie still seemed a little dozy when she came out into the living room, but she didn't appear ill. Still, I began to be uneasy about her. She did not respond when I called her name or talked to her; her ears didn't prick up nor did she look at me. I noticed that the pupils of her eyes were widely dilated. Was there something wrong with her eyes? I also wondered whether she was hearing me. Cats can be willfully "deaf," but this seemed different. We should undoubtedly pay Dr. Downey another visit.

That evening as Ed was sitting in his recliner reading I brought

Cassie

Cassie into the living room and set her on Ed's chair next to him, then returned to the kitchen where I had been working. A few minutes later Ed called out to me urgently, "I wonder if Cassie can see!" I quickly went back to the living room. Ed explained that Cassie had wanted to get down from the chair but had groped around its edge as if feeling for how far away the floor was.

Ed waved his hand in front of Cassie's eyes. No response. I looked into her face. Her hugely dilated pupils made her eyes look like little dark pools. She sat quietly, eyes open but unfocussed. "Cassie!" I said to her loudly though she was only a few feet from me. No response. I snapped my fingers. No reaction. I turned her face toward me, looked straight at her and called her name again. She felt my touch. She purred then, but otherwise did not respond. Then we knew the difficult truth: since sometime during the night from Saturday to Sunday Cassie had become both blind and deaf. I was bewildered. Ed fell silent.

I set Cassie on the floor; she sat down in place. We stared at her. When she did walk away she bumped into the coffee table. As she reached the living room doorway five or six feet away she cut her angle too short and bumped into the wall. She didn't hurt herself but watching her was distressing. Those bumps were not more than slight taps. At least her whiskers were in working order; there wasn't any chance she would get her head caught in a too-small space. But how could a cat with hyperthyroidism who was also both unseeing and unhearing have any kind of life?

I felt tension grow in my gut. It had often been hard to love Cassie the incessant whiner. But now I felt only compassion for her. Who wants to see their cat suffer, laden with such an onerous double handicap? Ironically, now that she had something serious to whine about she was quiet. She was almost eerily quiet – except for her purr: my touch reassured her, and whenever I picked her up or stroked her a few times where she stood on the floor she purred. That touched my heart. She was now enclosed in a tiny world, dark and silent, but she was relying on Ed and me. Touch and smell would be her only guides to this disconcerting new world.

We would call Dr. Downey immediately the next morning. But what to do, ultimately? The word *euthanasia* loomed. Again I asked myself: What kind of life can any animal species so reliant on sight and hearing have without those senses? What could it be like to be imprisoned in darkness and silence? And what about the hyper-thyroidism? Was it fair to keep such a cat alive, and for whose sake?

I had to try to find out what was going on. I went over to my computer and opened the browser. I typed "cause of deafness and blindness in cats" into Google. The first thing I found out was that Cassie's hyperthyroidism was clearly the underlying cause of both. The disease can cause severely high blood pressure. I had read that somewhere previously, but since it hadn't applied to Cassie – until now, apparently – I had simply shoved it from my mind. The hypertension can cause so much pressure in the head that it can detach the eyes' retinas, resulting in blindness. I had also read *that* somewhere before but hadn't paid much attention. Cassie had been fine on the medication she was taking.

That hyperthyroidism would cause both blindness and deafness was much more rare but not unheard of, I read on. Sometimes, if treatment were administered within a day or, at most, two after the onset of the blindness, the blindness would reverse, I learned. Cassie had become blind and deaf the previous night or early morning and I didn't yet know how soon we would get to see Dr. Downey. I wasn't hopeful about a reversal.

Then I found something that heartened me. There are people, quite a few of them, who own cats that are both deaf and blind; and those cats seemed to be having good lives. In compensation for the loss of sight and hearing the cats' senses of touch and smell became acute and they were living happily (their owners said). Perhaps this wasn't a death sentence for Cassie after all. We weren't about to banish her from our lives if she truly could have a decent life despite her profound handicaps.

It would be Tuesday afternoon before we could get a vet appointment. I didn't protest or consider bringing her to the emergency clinic as we later would Dancer when she had her first kidney crisis. The damage was done. In fact, Ed and I made sure we took an appointment we could go to together. It was still possible we might need to make the decision to have Cassie euthanized. I surely didn't want to make that decision alone, nor did Ed want me to, of course.

Dr. Downey confirmed that Cassie was both blind and deaf and that her blood pressure was dangerously high. (Cat blood pressure is taken just like human blood pressure, but with an appropriately tiny cuff.) He was sympathetic but I could tell that her sudden simultaneous loss of sight and hearing fascinated him from a medical point of view. I couldn't blame him. It *was* rare. But Cassie would very soon become an even more intriguing case.

We left with a prescription for a blood pressure medication and headed to our drugstore. As it was another human drug used for cats in minute proportions, Dr. D. didn't have any on hand. Cassie was to take it in addition to the methimazole. Late that afternoon she had her first dose.

Cassie was learning to negotiate her way around the house without bumping into things and she was a fast learner. She knew where everything was, of course, so navigating in the house was a matter of judging distances from one object and room to another. Still, I considered what life would be like for me were I unable to hear or see. Being a classical musician and life-long lover of music (never mind the need for hearing related to speech) I couldn't fathom being without my hearing; the silence would include, of course, never hearing Ed's voice again, nor any other voices. And were I blind I would deeply miss Ed's intelligent blue eyes and his smile. The world of nature, too, which we believe is God's exquisite creation and which Ed and I relish so, would be a closed book. Reading music would be impossible; and reading books and using the computer would be a real challenge. Granted, cats don't type or read. But our cats do love classical music on their catly level.

I was sorry that I hadn't, over the years, been able to feel the warmth for Cassie that I had for all our other cats, but that didn't prevent me from wanting her to have the best possible life. So since Sunday I had been praying for her, as I would pray for Dancer later and as I had prayed for Marple, Delta and Maple before her – God's creatures all. I boldly argued my case. I asked God to restore at least one of Cassie's senses so that she need not live in both darkness and silence. I reminded him of how lavishly he had endowed cats with exceptional characteristics, including their particular manner of using sight and hearing, and how difficult it must be for such an animal to be missing both of those senses. Unknown to me, but not surprising, Ed was also praying for Cassie. He later told me with a wry smile, "I prayed, 'O Lord, will you trade her eyes for her vocal chords?'"

We were to return Cassie to Dr. Downey in a week to see how she was doing and to have her blood pressure rechecked, as getting the right amount of medication in that regard, too, could be tricky. On Friday morning as I prepared the cats' breakfast I looked at Cassie. Her head was up, tilted in my direction. I looked again. Her pupils were of normal size.

"Cassie!" I called to her, staring straight at her. She blinked, walked over to me and rubbed my leg with her head. I put my hand down near her face and drew a large circle in front of her with my index finger. She followed the circle. I started to grin. Then I laughed. "Thank you, LORD!" I said out loud. "Thank you!"

I picked up Cassie. She purred. I put her down again to let her eat. The other cats set to their meals, oblivious. I now wondered about her hearing. "Hey, Cassie!" I called rather loudly. She looked up. *Oh, wow!* I said to myself, exhaling deeply. *She can hear too?* I was almost positive she could, though it was at first hard to tell whether it was only her renewed sight that was guiding her reactions. Nevertheless, a fragment of a Bible verse came to my mind instantly, about God giving us more than we can ask or imagine. I had asked for the renewal of one sense for Cassie but both seemed to have been restored. Over the next few days it became obvious that Cassie *could* hear, though perhaps not as acutely as before.

It was the medication, skeptics will say. Yes, the medication did lower her blood pressure. But Cassie had been blind and deaf for almost a week. Relieved pressure might allow retinas to reattach after a day, possibly two, but not a week. And there's little or no precedent for hearing returning in such a situation. When I brought Cassie back to Dr. Downey the following Tuesday, a week after he had first confirmed her loss of sight and hearing and 11 days after the onset of that loss he was astonished and delighted. "This cat has made medical history!" he exclaimed. "I've never seen this happen. I should write this up." *I think the blood pressure pills had a little help,* I said to myself. But I just smiled and said, "Yes, it's pretty amazing, isn't it."

The next time we brought Cassie to have her thyroid levels checked we didn't hear anything from the clinic. Dr. Downey himself routinely calls his clients to relay blood test results, so not hearing from him made us conclude that everything was ok. As it turned out, that wasn't so. One night more than a month later when I returned from a choir rehearsal Ed said, "Dr. Downey called. There was some mix-up about the results of Cassie's blood tests. Apparently they were sent to another vet and Downey just got them, finally. Cassie's thyroid is too active again. He wants us to start giving her a whole pill instead half when she gets her second dose of medication every day." So I began adding the daily extra half-pill the next day. That was a small warning of things to come that I chose to ignore.

Some weeks later as I was heading to the laundry room one afternoon I glanced at Cassie who was lying meatloaf style near the backdoor along the outer wall. The floor there is linoleum and along most of the length of the wall runs a hot-water baseboard register. It's a warm place, a favorite of all the cats during the cold months.

I looked again at Cassie, more carefully this time. I knew the meatloaf position could indicate some kind of discomfort, distress or pain. Her sides were heaving in and out noticeably and quickly. Her breathing was fast but shallow; she acted as if she were having a hard time getting enough air.

Something else was wrong now, and it seemed serious. We decided we had better bring Cassie to see Dr. Downey again, and right away. I called and explained the symptoms. This time I was able to get in quickly, but it would be during the day when Ed would not be able to be there.

The news wasn't good. Fluid had built up around Cassie's heart and in her lungs. She *was* having difficulty breathing. Dr. Downey talked about what an amazingly resilient cat Cassie had proved to be over the last year-and-a-half since her initial diagnosis of hyperthyroidism, and he marveled again at her regaining of sight and hearing. But this new thing was very serious; life-threatening, and Cassie had now begun to suffer. Despite her valiant fight, it might be time to ease her out of this life. Yet there was one possible alternative. We could try putting her on a diuretic, a "water pill," which might reduce the fluid enough to normalize her breathing and thus improve some other bodily functions.

Dr. D. could suggest reasonable options, but whatever the decision, we'd have to make it ourselves. This was 2008. Dancer was still alive and quite well (except for some arthritis). It was the first time in more than eight years – since Delta's death – that we had had to confront the possible loss of one of our cats (though it had already arisen in our minds when Cassie first became blind and deaf).

Dr. Downey gave me time to call Ed to discuss what we would do. I explained the options: possible life or certain death. At one point in that five-minute conversation we concluded it might be time to say good bye to Cassie. The thought of it brought tears to my eyes. As Ed and I talked further the tears spilled down my cheeks. I loved Cassie after all, and far more than I was aware.

There had been a remarkable change in her personality since the onset of her blindness and deafness and then the recovery of those senses. Upon their recovery she had remained the quiet cat she had become when she lost those senses. She now seemed cheerful in the way cats can exude that quality, and was even playful some of the time. For weeks she had emitted not the slightest whine, not even a slightly whiney meow. She only purred, and she did a great deal of that.

Ed and I agreed that we would not throw in the towel just yet. We would try this one last thing: the diuretic. Dr. D. said it would be obvious within a day, two at most, whether it was working. There wouldn't be long to wait and Cassie would not have to suffer long if it did not work.

When I had hung up and Dr. Downey returned to the room I told him what we had decided. "She's a tough cat. It's great she's going to get one more chance," he said cheerfully. He was clearly happy with our decision.

On the way home I drove straight to the pharmacy; as I drove I prayed for Cassie once again. There might be no future in this. The prescription was for only four pills. It was possible we would need less than one.

I had dropped down the back seats on my hatchback so that Cassie's carrier could rest on the resulting platform and be shoved up close to the front seats. That gave her a view (of sorts) of the area between the front seats; she could see me and I could look at her and talk to her at stoplights.

She now lay quietly in her carrier, seemingly unperturbed – or perhaps too ill to care – about this detour that would not allow us to go straight home. Her diuretic would be yet another human drug used for cats, her third. I would need to buy a pill cutter to divide each pill into quarters. One-quarter pill would be her cat-portion each day. How many such days did she have left?

I gave her her first quarter before supper along with her other two pills. By late that evening her sides heaved much less noticeably as she breathed. By the next morning she was breathing normally. I thanked God once again.

<u>Cassie</u>

We continued to give Cassie her three medicines. They were keeping her alive. Several months went by. We had Cassie's blood checked yet again and everything was as it should be. Except that in the meantime we lost Dancer: a very big "except that" which will reverberate a long time in our lives.

Oddly enough, just after we lost Dancer, Cassie went back to being a whiner for while, though it's not obvious to me that Dancer's death had much, if anything, to do with it. We really couldn't blame her. She had been through a lot. We took it to mean she was back to being her old self. And she was.

Cassie's expressing of her "old self" wasn't to last indefinitely. Five weeks after our enforced goodbye to Dancer, Cassie needed her blood checked again. She had gone silent again, but not happily so. She was lethargic once more. Worse, she had begun to pick at her food. When a cat loses its appetite it's never a good sign.

The results of the new round of blood tests left *us* silent with surprise. Cassie's kidneys were no longer working properly. Dr. Downey suspected that that had been the case for some time, but her medication had masked the symptoms. In plain language: Cassie had kidney disease in addition to the hyper-thyroid condition.

The ordeal we had so recently seen Dancer through came vividly, forcefully, to mind. "I just can't go through this again. Not in the same way!" I said emphatically, sorrowfully, to Ed. It was clear I also said it for him.

We decided then and there that once Cassie stopped eating altogether, as she surely would, we would not try to force-feed her as we had briefly (unsuccessfully) forced Dancer to eat. Nor would I try to feed her numerous times a day after pureeing and warming a few spoonfuls of food each time. Yes, we would haul out the paraphernalia of Dancer's we had put away: the potassium gel, the Astro's oil, a new bag of lactated ringers solution to administer subcutaneous injections. We would give her those injections every few evenings during the next week to see if that eased her discomfort and helped her appetite. We would give her whatever else she needed in terms of medication and supplements. But we would not go to the lengths we had with Dancer.

Dancer, despite her extreme illness, had continued to interact with us actively until the moment she died. But Cassie was withdrawing from us, from her feline family members, from life. Clearly she was now feeling miserable, and was maybe in pain. We just couldn't tell. She slept on our bed at night now, which she normally did only in winter; it was June 2009. She seemed to like the contact and warmth. And she still came into the kitchen now and then when she felt hungry. But when she got there she would eat very little, and what she did eat had to be especially palatable. I frequently opened new small cans of food in an effort to find a flavor that whetted her appetite. Beyond that minor activity she slept all day long on a windowsill in the sun or on our bed. And then all night long on our bed.

The next week Cassie fell into a dramatic downward spiral. Two times that week we did give her subcutaneous injections and they seemed to relieve her a bit. But she was now refusing to eat except the odd bite here and there when I had pureed the food. Yes, I had relented. Of course we didn't want to starve her or add to her suffering. We did give her potassium gel, as Dr. Downey prescribed; and we forced Astro's Oil down her throat a few times. But she continued to deteriorate and by Tuesday night had stopped purring in response to being petted. She having been an inordinate purrer all her life, I knew that that was a serious sign. The next day she spent on our bed, and the next, when she ate nothing.

Her eyes were becoming increasingly glassy (I suspected she now had a serious headache from high blood pressure). She was sinking into another world. We could bring her in on Friday at 4:00. Dr. Downey himself would not be there; a young recent vet-school graduate who he had just hired would attend to things.

When it was nearly time to leave home, I went to the bedroom to get Cassie. She wasn't there. I began to look into all the corners and crevices in the house that were favorite spots of hers. I couldn't find her. My alarm gradually grew. I had heard stories of cats, knowing they were going to die, crawling off into a remote corner to get on with it. Some 10 minutes later I finally found her on the floor on the far side of our bed, facing the bed. She looked as if she were about to crawl under it. The events of the next hour made me think that my hunch about her intent may have been right.

On the 20-minute trip to the vet Cassie occupied the same basket Dancer had, lined with a fresh blanket. Seven weeks and one day had passed since we had made that trip with Dancer. But unlike Dancer,

94

Cassie

Cassie was not interested in looking out the window. She barely moved and made no sound except two loud whines – welcome cries just then – as she stood up and turned around in the basket.

I petted her and talked softly to her. I began to feel the faint vibration of a purr under my hand as I caressed her soft fur. In response I leaned down and put my ear to her back to see if I could actually hear it. I could! It surprised and cheered me immensely.

When we arrived we petted Cassie and talked to her as we waited. Then a vet tech we often saw there took her into the back to insert the catheter into which the overdose of anesthetic would be administered. "I'll bring her back in just a minute," the tech said, and indeed, with Dancer that procedure had taken not more than a minute. But now minute after minute passed and the tech did not return with Cassie.

"What's taking them so long? Where's Cassie?" I asked Ed in agitation as he sat next to me, as if he would know. The young vet was at the other end of the waiting room talking with an elderly couple about their cat's necessary dental work. The door to the back opened suddenly and we heard, "Doctor, we need you!" Ed and I looked at each other quizzically and with some apprehension. Almost five more minutes passed. Then we were finally led into the same room where we and Dancer had spent *her* last minutes.

Cassie lay in her basket on her side, the catheter bandage wrapped around one of her front legs, I don't remember which one. She was unconscious. Though her eyes were open they were unseeing. We tried to quickly take in what was going on but were confused about what had happened. "As we put the catheter in she crashed," we were told. I must have asked if she was dead, I don't actually remember. I only heard, as if from a distance, "Her heart is still beating."

I didn't know exactly what "crashed" meant, nor did Ed. He was silent and look worried. I began to ask questions, then, trying to grasp why Cassie was lying there like that, uncomprehending, when we had wanted to hold her and reassure her when the time came to administer that fateful needle.

Whatever "crashed" meant medically, in practicality it meant that Cassie had essentially chosen her own time to die. The caresses and reassurances we had given her on the trip there and in the waiting room would forever have to suffice as our goodbye.

When we returned home we set Cassie's basket down on the living room floor and pulled back the blanket that had covered her. Given the surprising way the other cats had responded in agitation and almost fear to Dancer's body, we wondered, uneasy, what their reaction would be now.

It was altogether different. Though Cassie was a year younger than Digory and Caspian, she had been a kind of mother-figure for them. They had known her for 12 years, all her life in our home. They had groomed each other, slept together and watched the squirrels and birds together. And now, it was as if they were holding a wake for her, joined by Keeley and Roo, too. Rather than having to bodily carry each cat to the basket, they all gathered round. One at a time they sniffed and looked, then sat next to the basket; then sniffed and looked and sat again. Five minutes passed before, one by one, they began to walk away. Digory was the last one to leave; he had been the closest to Cassie.

For the next few days all four remaining cats seemed to need more attention than usual, and the more so Digory and Caspian. As Cassie had become sicker they had withdrawn from her, and she from them. We had seen that disconcerting aspect of cat behavior before. But Roo's behavior had been touching. She had again played nurse-maid, though not to the extent she had done with Dancer.

When Digory, Caspian, Keeley and Roo had finished with their goodbyes, we buried Cassie under the apple tree next to Dancer. In seven weeks the blossoms had grown into small, bright green apples. I picked a twig containing several healthy leaves and a nicely shaped miniature fruit and laid it on top of Cassie's body bag before we replaced the earth. It was another lovely sunny day, if another dispiriting one for us.

Six days after that black Friday I talked with Dr. Downey, who had naturally been briefed on what had happened. He suggested that the renewed fluid build-up that had made Cassie's breathing difficult, no doubt along with the stress of the trip and being handled by people she didn't know, was too big a strain on her over-worked heart.

Cassie was 13 years old, not terribly old for a cat. In some ways she had had a tough life; certainly that was so off and on in her last few years. There's no doubt that Cassie's permanent absence will leave a renewed and painful tear in the fabric of our feline-human household. And, indeed, the house seemed rather empty with our two feline *grand dames* gone. It had been many years since we had only four cats.

Cassie's unexpected patience in adversity – not the long years of pushy whining – is what Ed and I will remember most about her. And that's a very fine memory to have of a beautiful little mother cat who we took in one August day when she desperately needed a home.

Cassie with Digory

6. Keeley: The Big Lad with the Tiny Voice

Keeley

In the summer of 2003 we still lived in Lewiston in our first house. It would be nearly two years before we would move, though we were already talking about the possibility. Constantly climbing and descending the stairs to our bedroom and to the laundry room in the basement was getting to be a burden for Ed. I even wondered if he might be starting to exhibit signs of post-polio syndrome, but he, understandably, didn't want to think of that. Yet. (He had been six years old when polio struck, three years before the vaccine had first been used on the public.)

But Ed *was* willing to talk about our future need for a house without stairs, a nice one-story ranch, perhaps, with the laundry room as well as everything else on ground level. If we started looking soon, we could take our time and not buy another house unless it exactly suited us and our budget. That would also put us in a better position to sell our existing house, we reasoned. The housing market was modest-to-terrible in western New York, but we just wouldn't worry about that. (In fact, that meant that the extreme highs and lows that effected many other real estate

98

markets just didn't happen where we lived.) If we could pray about something so "insignificant" as a cat, surely our future housing needs also qualified, and those prayers would be answered, we believed. (And that indeed became the case.)

By 2003, Caspian was eight years old, Digory was almost eight, Dancer was 10 and Cassie was seven. Marple, Delta and Maple had all been gone from our lives for what seemed like ages: Delta for three years, Maple and Marple for eight years.

There was a time – when we contemplated getting Dancer, as I've noted – when having *three* cats seemed like the surest example of insanity on our part. But three had turned out to make a fine feline family and was no more work than two: just put down another food bowl and another litter box. We had long since gotten past that hurdle. In fact, for the three years from Cassie's arrival to our enforced farewell to Delta we had had *five*. A serious case of cataholism if there ever was one!

What caused us to suddenly look for another cat three years after Delta died I'm not entirely sure. I do know that my confessed weakness for handsome tabbies played a large role. As did my impeccable logic: if four made a quite workable, happy feline family just as well as three did, then surely five would work just as well as four, as it had before.

On Saturday mornings Ed and I sleep in a bit then have a leisurely breakfast. We linger over coffee while we read our regional newspaper and the local freebie centered on Lewiston and vicinity. In that latter paper there was a column advertising lost and found pets, pets available for adoption, and so on. And sometimes when the Rainbow Shelter had an especially large population, to spur people to adopt pets the shelter would post pictures and sentence-long descriptions of cats or dogs that needed homes.

One Saturday in August as we read the papers my eye caught two cat photos in that column. I have no hint of memory about what that second cat looked like, but I was smitten with the tabby kitten looking perkily out at me from the newsprint. He had huge tall ears for the size of his small head, and bright inquisitive eyes. The photo was black-and-white so I couldn't tell his coloring but I guessed he had a bit more gray in him than Digory does, or than Caspian's built-in blanket does.

I showed the picture to Ed. Of course he agreed the kitten was cute. How could he not? But he wasn't keen on going over to the shelter to look at the little creature. This time around, it seemed, Ed would need some coaxing. I can't remember what line of reasoning (or cajoling) I used to convince him (I wish I could in case I ever need it again). But whatever argument I made, it worked. And Ed found himself on the way to the Rainbow Shelter with me.

The kitten was nearly five months old. He was a delightful creature, friendly and cheerful despite his having been locked in a small cage for who-knew-how-long. He was wriggly when first I, then Ed, picked him up. He had plenty of pent-up energy. He needed to get out of that cage for good, and soon. Though it was obvious he enjoyed being petted he had to be coaxed to purr; when he finally did it was subtle, the only subtle thing about this boisterous kitten.

I was right about his coat. There was a grayish-silvery cast to it along with the tabby browns, tans and blacks. He did not have the defined and obvious spots and stripes Digory has. His black stripes were more muted and truncated, shorter in length and smaller in circumference. They tended to blend into the ticked fur that covered most of his body. His forehead "M," too, was small and not well defined; the two sections of the M were broken apart, one over each eye, like upside down V's. He had the tabby-typical narrow black stripes on each side of his head, running outward sideways from his eyes. The narrow rings of fur immediately around his eye lids were tan and his chin was snowy white, as were his whiskers.

A thick black line ran the length of his back and all the way to the tip of his tail, though it gradually blended with the ticked fur. While Digory has a clearly defined diamondback rattlesnake pattern running the length of his tail, this kitten's tail showed some tabby rings, but they partially melded into the other fur on his tail. His tail! What a magnificent appendage it was. I marveled to see that it was actually longer than the rest of his body.

This kitten had big feet too. I had read somewhere that that meant he would be a big cat. Yet he seemed only moderate-sized for being nearly five months old, so perhaps that was an old wives' tale and he would be only a moderate-sized adult like Digory instead of a large tom like Caspian.

If we wanted him – we did! – we could pick him up in three days after he had been neutered. The operation would be included in the adoption fee. So three days later I drove back to the shelter to get him (Ed was still at work). I put the kitten in the carrier that rested on the passenger seat beside me. He wasn't keen on the car ride. He was nervous and cried anxiously in a high-pitched kitten way. His tiny voice made me smile.

I wondered whether he associated car rides with negative things. I talked to him, and at a stoplight was able to put my hand in the carrier to pet him for a moment. Both the talking and petting settled him down. He was still likely a little sore from his operation as well. His distressed cries weren't surprising.

That night at the supper table Ed and I talked about a name for the kitten. We agreed it wouldn't be another Narnian name this time. How about something Irish, after Ed's heritage? Could we find something meaningful, musical sounding but also pronounceable? I checked through a list of Irish names on the Internet and wrote some of them down. We tried out several but didn't like them; several others seemed contrived, or just not appropriate for a cat. Then we came to "Keeley." The name was said to mean "handsome." We would take their word for it. If that's what it meant it certainly was appropriate, it had a nice two-syllable lilt, that strong initial K, and there was no problem saying the word. Keeley it would be.

Once again we also went through our introduce-a-new-cat routine. We wondered how our adult males would react to this young male. We need not have worried. They readily accepted him. Cassie, too, took his presence in stride. Dancer didn't mind him but, as Dancer required, made him keep his distance. When he exuberantly ran up to her and wanted to touch noses she backed him away with a hiss and an up-raised paw. After a couple of such encounters he learned not to invade her personal space. Soon, though, he was curling up with Caspian, Digory and Cassie in a foursome heap.

That continued for four or five months until Keeley had grown a great deal. The big feet he had at five months old did tell a story. Keeley was becoming a very large cat. He would be bigger than Caspian – about the same length but taller and broader. He had more than caught up with his magnificent tail. And he began to feel his strength. One evening he took a run at Digory and pounced. He was testing his own prowess, and Digory's, to see if he could "take" Digory. It was the start of an ongoing play for dominance. Digory was not impressed and fought Keeley off easily.

The spat sounded far more serious than it was. Digory can spit and yowl almost as impressively as Dancer could. But Keeley's kittenish yelling made us laugh. To this day, at six years old, he has a high, kitten-like meow that I think of as the cat equivalent of a boy soprano. A more accurate description in musical terms, however, would be soprano castrato! The tiny voice and the large male cat are humorously incompatible.

As time went on Keeley would periodically re-attempt to get the better of Digory. Over time he became gradually more successful. For a while I thought that Keeley may have risen above Digory in rank, though Caspian was still the benign overall ruler of the three. Laid-back Caspian saw no threat in Keeley, and Keeley made no attempt to test Caspian's dominance. They, in fact, began to be very good friends.

Digory would also periodically make *his* move against Keeley. When he initiated a fight with Keeley he wasn't careful to sheath his claws. His intent was serious: this young punk needed to be taught a lesson. The lesson accomplished, the two would go back to being friends, more or less. But now, Keeley and Digory are no longer the buddies they were when Keeley was a kitten and no threat to Digory. And they are not the kind of friends that Keeley and Caspian (and Caspian and Digory) still are. Keeley and Digory still go through cycles of sparring then observing a truce. It is not unlikely that one future day Keeley will become top cat. Caspian has already begun to acquiesce to what Keeley wants, though it's entirely voluntary and there's never any fighting about it.

Once Keeley was full grown and a couple of years old he still regularly interacted with Caspian, Digory and Cassie, but he also grew to need his own space, rather like Dancer did. He wasn't so much a loner as simply a cat who came to enjoy time and space to himself.

When we moved, Keeley was especially intrigued by the new sights and sounds outside the patio doors, the back doors and my home-office windows. He would sit for an hour or more at a time staring out a window here, another there, a door over there. Then he'd snooze for a while, and repeat his nature watch. Snooze, watch, snooze, watch. After a while he claimed a spot on a folded towel laid on top of a two-drawer file cabinet under the bank of three double-hung windows in my office. That became his domain.

Keeley

The year of this writing, four years after we moved and as Keeley is six years old, his personality has suddenly blossomed in an unexpected way. During the winter past he began hopping up on our bed at night, sleeping next to my feet. In all the previous time in our current house Keeley would sleep in the other end of the house on his filing cabinet, where the windows next to him let him keep tabs on the outside world even through the night, if he wished. He still does that, but now he's much more amenable to company.

Also in the last year Keeley finally decided that being caressed and petted is one of his life's greatest pleasures. Before that, we wondered. He usually liked attention when we gave it, but he almost never sought it out himself, and when Ed or I approached him to pet him, after not many seconds he would disengage himself and run away; literally run away, usually to another room. We decided that he was hyper-sensitive to sensory stimulation, as some cats are, and could not tolerate more. I had read about that phenomenon and concluded that it fit Keeley. If we were to pet him just a bit too long he would bite the hand that was petting him – usually gently, but bite nevertheless; or he would "embrace" that hand in all four paws, claws partially extended.

But now we seem to have a new Keeley. Not only does he seek out our bed when we're in it (a cynic might argue he's just looking for warmth when the temperature drops at night), but he seeks affection and closeness in other ways. Often of a morning he will jump up on my nightstand then reach over and nudge my shoulder, arm or face with his nose. He knows that in response to that signal a hand will reach out to *him* and ruffle the fur on his forehead, scratch the fur on his nose or massage his whole head. And his response to that is a loud, rattley purr. Yes, he has learned to purr at last, and he does it more and more frequently and loudly. He'll even stay on the bed and allow Ed to pet him for several minutes at a time.

He now also loves to go into the bathroom, plop down on the bath rug and let me scratch his stomach – not too long, but he'll allow it nonetheless. In our house, that kind of sudden and spontaneous self-removal of a cat's legs from underneath its body is referred to as the Delta Flop. Delta was our first cat to routinely do that when she wanted belly scratching or petting. When Caspian does the Delta Flop, unlike Keeley, he goes into a near catatonic state (no pun intended) while having his belly scratched. Every muscle relaxes, his eyes close, and he would stay in that position indefinitely if either Ed or I had the fortitude to scratch and pet him indefinitely. Keeley is more reserved about it, but now clearly loves it, nonetheless.

Keeley has another trick he's been trying lately. We use the door that leads from my office to our deck as the main door to the deck (there are also the french doors from the living room to the deck). When Keeley is in the mood to explore he lies in wait for me to go in or out. This happens most often around supper time in summer, as the grill is nearby; or on Saturday mornings if Ed and I are eating breakfast outside, as we often do.

Keeley periodically tries to shoot out the door as soon as it opens. When we go in or out we're always on the alert for cats hanging around that door or any other door we're going to use, but inevitably he's successful once in a while – enough to encourage him to keep trying. Once outside he sprints around the yard like a mad greyhound. He'll stop for a half-minute or so to nibble on some pond grass; then he darts away again. No matter how wily I am or nonchalant I act when trying to reel him in, I can't catch him if he doesn't want to be caught. He could be a direct descendent of Marple's.

Occasionally he ventures into the next yard, at the back of which there is catnip growing. I myself planted a large terra cotta pot of catnip this spring, though Keeley hasn't noticed it. But when I pick a leaf for each of the cats, bring the leaves inside and tear each in half to release the scent of the oil in them, every one of the cats goes hyperactively berserk. They each eat the leaves as fast as possible, roll on the floor and beg for more.

I'm not concerned that Keeley will run away when he gets out. Because his senses are so continually stimulated when he's outside he tires easily. Within five minutes he'll let me approach him, pick him up and deposit him back into the house.

When Keeley gets out, however, potential mutiny stirs. Caspian and Digory take great exception. *Why is he out and we're not?* their eyes and demeanor say to me accusingly. So several times on a Saturday morning when Keeley has escaped I've simply let them out too for a few minutes, keeping a careful eye on them. It's never difficult to round them up and bring them back inside. Cassie was sometimes interested in going out, but not often. And Roo, having been a stray not that terribly long ago, still seems to have a love-hate relationship with the great outdoors. When she wants to be outside with us, one of us holds her in our lap, and that generally lasts two minutes or less.

After Cassie's death and the arrival of Hedwig, Keeley welcomed her in his gregarious, rambunctious way. She's an affectionate, friendly cat, but she's shy and cautious, and hasn't relished being kissed by this big galoot of a cat who is far bigger and taller than she. When she arrived and Keeley almost immediately tried to touch noses with her in his affable manner, she backed him off with a hiss. He got the message, but it didn't faze him. A few days later, he approached her again in the same manner. That time his effort was rewarded; she returned the nose-touch greeting. Keeley has that effect on his fellow cats (except Digory). They soon seem to understand his happy intent and that, big as he is, he's a thoroughly harmless, good-natured creature.

Keeley's main contribution to our feline mix has been a cheerful and goofy rambunctiousness. It is a dimension of cathood that only Keeley has exhibited. And now that we've seen it, we cherish it; and the more so the crazy, increasingly affectionate cat who has uniquely shown us that quality.

Young Keeley getting a bath from Caspian

7. Roo: The Ugly Duckling

Roo

The evening of August 11, 2006, was warm, though not so humid as many evenings earlier in the summer had been. Later in August the evenings would be cool enough that long sleeves might be needed and the sliding patio door would be closed. But on August 11 that door was open and a pleasant breeze filtered through the screen.

Ed and I were both in the other part of the living room about 10 feet from the door, our backs to it. The five cats – Dancer, Caspian, Digory, Cassie and Keeley – were lounging here and there, most of them on the rug near the door, enjoying the breeze. Suddenly there was a commotion. I heard what I thought was a plaintive meow from a cat I didn't recognize. At the sound, our cats instantly went on high alert, creating their own ruckus. All five began converging on the screen door.

I quickly got up to see what was going on. The cats parted to let me get to the door. Looking up at me was the most pitifully emaciated, ugly feline creature I had ever seen. Her starving body made her head look huge. Her feet, too, appeared gigantic. Her fur was dirty and matted. As I

106

scrutinized her I could see that what looked like mats were odd blotches of dull and dingy color. Instantly a picture of Dobby the house elf in the Harry Potter stories appeared before me and I involuntarily smiled. The condition of this little creature, though, was no laughing matter.

She had not backed away as our five cats had moved toward the screen, nor did she when she saw me approach. When she saw me looking at her she meowed again. It was no friendly greeting. It was a cry for help, a cry of desperation and hunger. I realized that, earlier in the day, the animal I had thought was a squirrel, which had come uncharacteristically close to the house and had streaked away when I had moved toward the door, must have been this starving young cat.

She didn't intend to run this time. She boldly disregarded the five pairs of cat eyes staring her down from the other side of the screen. She planted herself two feet from the screen and the staring cats and half meowed, half yowled. As I moved up next to the screen and reached toward its lock she moved even closer to her side of the door. Oh, how she wanted to come in and eat! Her desperation gave her courage.

Ed came up behind me then to take a look. "See how emaciated she is," I said. "We need to feed her." It was something we never did but he concurred. We quickly decided that we would feed her in the garage. We would put a towel in a cardboard box for her and let her stay there for the night. Then in the morning we would call Niagara Feline Friends, a local no-kill shelter. She had surely already had enough trouble in her young life.

I managed to slip out the screen door without any of our cats getting out. When I stooped to pick up the young cat she readily allowed it. I walked around the house with her to the garage, which Ed had already opened.

Once we had re-closed the door I set her on the floor. She wanted to follow me into the house. When I returned with a quarter-cup of dry cat food in a bowl she smelled it from the other side of the garage where she had been nosing around after I went into the house. She bounded over and nearly ran up my jeans leg to get at the bowl. We had sometimes joked about Caspian and Keeley inhaling their food, while Digory, Cassie and Dancer were nibblers. This cat might be a nibbler some day but not right then. She did nearly inhale the food. And in the next moment she looked up at me as if to say, "Isn't there more?" I didn't want to make her ill, but I did get a little more and she ate that just as fast as the first quarter cup. Then she drank some of the water I put down for her. Being not quite so famished she now began to look at me, Ed, and her surroundings again. We petted her, then I showed her her bed for the night and left the garage.

When I carried her to the garage I had noticed a pungent, unpleasant smell about her. Cats, even strays, don't normally smell bad, so the strong odor was unusual. I wondered if it were a discharge from her nether region but that part of her had seemed clean, unlike her dull and ugly fur. This young thing wasn't going to win any feline beauty contests, that was sure.

Our cats congregated in the hallway between the kitchen and the interior garage door. They seemed more curious and excited than perturbed. I was surprised. The usual behavior when a neighbor's cat or a rare stray intruded on our yard – or worse, onto the deck – was growling, hissing, fur standing on end and a frightful howling by Cassie that would make anyone who didn't know her (or us) think she was simultaneously being tortured and experiencing a haunting.

In the morning I immediately called the woman who ran Feline Friends. She was sorry but she absolutely could not take one more cat right now, she said. Someone had just dumped four feline mothers with kittens, 24 cats in all. I sighed. I was reluctant to call the Rainbow Shelter. We had gotten Dancer, Caspian and Keeley there, but you never really knew whether someone else would adopt a stray you brought in, or whether that stray would forfeit its life for having been caught.

Fortunately for me, Ed was working in his office at home that morning so we could discuss what to do next. It began to look like we would have to consider keeping the stray, and we would have to make the decision quickly. It would be an act of charity. Would anyone but committed cataholics want to adopt such a repulsive, smelly, scrawny – and downright ugly – creature? We agreed we would call Dr. Downey and get the stray checked out. Even as we did so we were still considering bringing her to a shelter.

Roo

When I stepped inside the garage to feed the ugly duckling she ran right up to me, meowing urgently. This meow was not quite so desperate, but she was still famished. I let her eat, then picked her up. The nasty smell about her was now almost overwhelming. I had to find out where it was coming from.

I held her under her limbs, up high in front of me like a cat show judge, examining her from every angle. Then I saw it. Under her chin, on the front of her neck, was an open wound at least the size of a quarter. I could see what looked like a tendon at the edge of that open hole. The wound was not bleeding but oozed pus. Perhaps she had been torn by barbed wire or bitten by some other animal. That awful smell was the stench of infected flesh.

I went back into the house to tell Ed what I had discovered. This made matters more pressing. In fact, it clinched the stray's future. With such a wound she wouldn't last half-an-hour at any shelter that euthanized animals. She would be quickly and efficiently put out of her misery. Our choice was not much of a choice: allow that to happen and say it was for the best, or adopt her and get her the vet care she would need, and get it fast. No animal already severely malnourished could fight off that kind of infection indefinitely.

I called Dr. Downey's office once more, explained what we had just found and asked if there was any chance we could bring the stray in sooner than four days from now, our original appointment time. There was: we could bring her in early that afternoon, before Dr. D. saw his already scheduled clients for the day. We stuffed a clean towel into one of our carriers, loaded the stray into it and were at the clinic at exactly the appointed time.

The stray was astonishingly lively for having so severe a wound and for having used up her fat reserves weeks earlier. But she held quite still while Dr. Downey examined her mouth, took her temperature, checked for fleas and ear mites, palpated her belly and took a long look at the gaping hole in her neck.

Amazingly, she had no evidence of fleas or ear mites. The wound was an abscess probably caused, as I had thought, by a bite or barbed wire. Surgery would be required to clean it out and sew it up. And there was one more thing: she was pregnant, though near the beginning of her gestation period. I had guessed she was about nine months old; Dr. Downey said perhaps a year, though she was quite small – perhaps she hadn't grown much because she had been starving. She had been finding just enough food to keep her alive, but not more.

To our surprise Dr. D. said he had time to operate on her that very moment. He would fix the wound and spay her at the same time. She would need to stay overnight and would then need some recuperation time, but she would likely be ok after that, he thought. This sad little cat would not come cheap.

How much money should we or could conscientiously spend on the healthcare of our pets, and in the stray's case, a sorry-looking potential pet? That is an issue Ed and I have always seen as an important one for ourselves as Christians. But doing away with animals, willy-nilly, because you don't want to spend money to keep them healthy is also a serious moral matter, we feel. "A righteous man cares for the needs of his animals," says Proverbs 12:10. Yet spending hundreds or even thousands to keep terminally ill animals alive a little longer for the owners' sake may be a sin of excess, especially if it means that that money is diverted from family necessities or charitable causes.

This stray was not such a case, however. Despite her emaciation she was a tough, strong young cat with a specific injury that could be corrected. (And in any case we would have had her spayed.) She was certainly not feral, so it was unlikely she would have serious behavior problems. The way she related to us and Dr. Downey showed she had been born in the vicinity of people and had been handled by people very early. She was wild only in the sense of being unmannerly, but that was to be expected. She had been fending for herself, likely for quite a while.

Ed and I didn't need long to consult together. We told Dr. Downey to go ahead. This sickly, ugly little runt would be our sixth cat. *In for a penny, in for a pound.* She had somehow already gotten under our skin though we barely knew her. Her arrival at our door had seemed so peculiar. There were seldom strays in our neighborhood; neighbors' cats came by now and then, but rarely a stray, and when one did come through the yard or onto the deck we had normally already been seeing it for a while elsewhere; then it would disappear, never to be seen again. But this stray had materialized as if out of nowhere. No one else in the neighborhood had seen her (news about wandering cats always travels fast in our neighborhood where there are many cat lovers). She had specifically, resolutely, appeared in our yard and at our door as if something or Someone had whispered to her, "Go *there*. They'll save you."

The day after the stray's surgeries, we returned to the clinic. The abscess had been even larger and deeper than it looked. It had taken quite some time to clean it out, but all had gone well. Nor would she ever have kittens. (I felt a twinge of guilt about having had an already pregnant cat spayed, but there was no real option.)

The little cat would be in pain for a while. We took her home, renewed her box bed in the garage with one of the clean fleece blankets we use only for the cats, gently laid her in it, refilled the food and water bowls and went into the house. We judged that it would not be a good idea to immediately bring her in, even if only to the holding chamber for new cats, the guest bedroom.

She made no protest when we left her. She was still in pain and needed rest. She would have to try to find a comfortable position: she was wearing a plastic "Elizabethan" collar to prevent her from pawing or biting the stitches on her neck and belly. The collar looked huge. The only part of this scrawny little cat that was of normal size was her feet, but even those didn't look normal. Her hind feet, particularly, appeared gigantic in proportion to her bony, underdeveloped body. And though her head was large in comparison to her emaciated body, it had appeared to recede into normalcy when surrounded by the outsized cone-shaped collar she now wore.

The other cats once again began to stand watch at door leading to the garage, but as they became used to the stray's scent they gradually accepted it as normal and mostly lost interest. They regained interest as the stray healed and several days later began to meow at the door and snoop around the garage for new things to look at, smell and keep herself occupied.

The weight and circumference of the Elizabethan collar prevented her from walking normally; her head swayed from side to side as she moved and the collar occasionally scraped the floor. She simply accommodated to it, as she had to all other problems she had encountered in her young life. She made no attempt to rid herself of it as I had seen other cats and dogs do. Perhaps she had already tried that and found it hopeless.

When we brought the stray to Dr. Downey we hadn't chosen a name for her. Ed wanted Peeve, as in, our pet Peeve. I appreciated the pun but argued that it wasn't a great name for a cat. Besides, what if she happened to turn out to be really likeable? (We had often joked that Peeve should have been Cassie's name.)

Now that she was home and about to move into the guest bedroom and then into the feline family we needed to get on with naming her for real. I picked her up, hoping that holding her would conjure up a name. My right hand held her under her arm pits, my left hand supported her large back feet. She faced outward with her back against my chest because of the collar. "Her big back feet make her look like a kangaroo," I observed to Ed. He laughed. "She looks like she could hop eight or 10 feet in one spring." We had hit on it: we would call her Roo, short for kangaroo.

We soon discovered that Roo is the kind of name that allows for numerous fun and funny variations. Besides Kangaroo, Buckaroo has become the most common of them. When I call, "Buckaroo!" the now almost tubby former stray comes running, unless she's preoccupied with something more important, of course. That's seldom the case because she has learned that when I call her I will either have an empty yogurt dish she may lick clean (she's a butter and home-made yogurt addict) or I will want to initiate a game of catch-and-fetch with a plastic bottle cap or the plastic ring that previously sealed a vitamin bottle. Those rings are now Roo's most cherished toys. After the cost of her initial surgeries and vaccinations, she's been a cheap date.

Kangabuckaroo is one of my variations on her name, and Rooskey and Rooskey Dooskey are two of Ed's. (We recently found out that there's a village in Ireland called Rooskey.) Punkin' Roo is another nickname (chanted in a little two-phrase ditty with the phrases separated by syncopated-rhythm sound effects: *Punkin' Roo, Punkin' Roo* [simulated syncopated drum-brush sounds]; *We love you, we love you* [same simulated syncopated drum-brush sounds].

Ed, in his unique way, came up with a real song for Roo, more elaborate than his pseudo-German folk ditty for Dancer. Little Lulu (Lulu

Moppet) was a *Saturday Evening Post* comic strip that ran for nearly a decade from early 1935 to the end of 1944. Ed's not that old; he got to know Little Lulu during his childhood in the 1950s when the character was used in magazine ads for Pepsi and in Kleenex TV commercials on the "Perry Como Show." Then Little Lulu got her own cartoon show. The song that accompanied the show begins: *Little Lulu, Little Lulu, with freckles on her chin,/Always in and out of trouble, but mostly always in.* The refrain says: *Little Lulu, we love you-lu just the same, the same, little Lulu we love you-lu just the same.*

You can see where this is leading. The song under Ed's treatment has become, "Little Roo-lu, little Roo-lu...." Over the years every one of our cats has enjoyed music – particularly classical, which is almost exclusively what they hear. (If cows give more milk when listening to Mozart, as several studies have shown, surely Herr Mozart makes cats more content.) Each of our cats has also been fond of being sung to. We discovered within a week of taking her home that Roo particularly responds to singing, which is surely why we instinctively began to sing to her more and more often. Her ears prick up or swivel back (if the singer is behind her), and, uncannily, she very often meows in a distinctive way near the end of "Little Roo-lu," at the same spot each time.

When Carly Simon wrote her song, "I bet you think this song is about you," she clearly didn't own a cat like Roo. The song *would have been* about such a cat. The persona singing the song would likely have been better off with a pet like Roo than with the arrogant guy to whom she addressed the song ("You're so vain, I bet you think this song is about you"). If some cats do seem vain, Roo is not one of them. The early life that left her homeless and starving has made her relish human attention and affection and want to please us, her rescuers.

Perhaps that's why she interacts with Ed and me more intensely and more often than any of our other cats do. She and Ed have great fun together and she comes to him early every morning for "a petting down," as he calls it. She purrs ecstatically at having her nose rubbed, for many minutes at a time. When she wants us to get involved in her play with one of her rings, she'll recover one that she previously stashed away somewhere, then emit an urgent meow not unlike Caspian's hunting meow. She picks up the ring in her mouth, trots over to Ed's chair with it, drops it and looks up at him. As he picks it up she tenses, ready to spring after it when he throws it towards the living room doorway and into the foyer. The living room and hallway floors are hardwood and the foyer floor is slate, good materials for a running cat to slide on as she hurtles in to catch her prey. In her case it's not obvious whether or not she sees it as prey, as Caspian clearly does the towels he drags around on his night-time prowls. She loves the game itself. She'll fetch the ring over and over, rest a few minutes when she tires, then begin again.

None of our cats are a few hairs short of a coat when it comes to intelligence (though Caspian can be dozy and Ed jokes that his mama must have dropped him on his head as a kitten). But Roo is especially smart, at least as smart as Dancer was. In fact, Roo learned one of her skills from observing Dancer: how to sit just so and look at me just right to get me to turn on a trickle of water in the bathtub so that she can mess with the water (and occasionally drink some). Roo is now the only one that hones that talent, though Keeley sometimes watches inquisitively as Roo balances on the edge of the tub, stretches to get her mouth under the tap and snaps at the water playfully.

Roo has also observed from Digory's pawing at the frame of the screen door that that will get her our attention (though of a negative kind). Digory figured out that if he keeps pawing the *frame* of the screen (and if the screen is unlocked), he can pry it open, escape to the yard and allow the others to follow. And all that without damaging the screen. Smart as Roo is, the distinction between the screen and its frame is lost on her. Now and then if we're sitting outside and she thinks she wants to join us, she sinks her claws into the screen itself, earning her a well-placed squirt of water from the disciplinary spray bottle. No doubt that's why she doesn't try it often.

We have put her on a halter and leash only once and have carried her outside just a few times when she has acted like she wanted to join us outside. But she doesn't quite know what to do once she's out there. The big wide world is now foreign and scary to her. It's as if she doesn't remember her former life as a stray. Or perhaps she does all too well. She instinctively wants to explore but it frightens her. Even as we hold her she experiences sensory overload not unlike Keeley does. Every muscle tightens and she tires out within a few minutes. She's far happier inside (and we would never let her roam) yet the out-of-doors continues to fascinate her. Every warm afternoon she lies in a window sill in my office, where she is lying this very moment. The bottom edge of the row of three double-hung windows in the exterior wall next to my desk begins at three feet from the ground. Roo (like all the cats) has a front-row view of the bird feeder barely eight feet from the wall, a feeder continually visited by chipmunks, squirrels, the occasional rabbit and many bird species.

The other cats adjusted well to Roo. She was a baby in their terms. There was no question that she was at the bottom of the social totem pole and thus no threat to any of the others. But I'm also convinced that they sensed, as cats always do among themselves, that she was hurting, so they left her alone. She had to wear the Elizabethan collar for almost six weeks and could not have defended herself very well while in that contraption if one of the other cats had taken a run at her. None of them ever did. Roo gradually began running through the hall-ways, head swaying while trying to balance that huge collar, the collar now and then bouncing off the floor just as it had when she was staying in the garage. Three weeks into her collar-wearing routine I

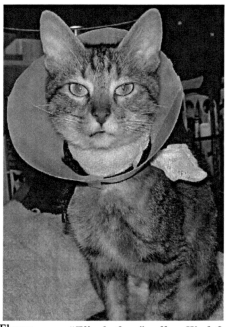

"Elizabethan" collar, Week 3

helped her out by cutting it down some, snipping off about an inch-and-a-half of the plastic on its outer edge. That made it somewhat less unwieldy. The more Roo healed, the happier and livelier she became.

Roo and Keeley decided immediately that they liked each other, and they became playmates. Three years on, Keeley picks fights with Roo now and then in his oafish, big-galoot way. Often, she takes exception to his attentions. He merely wants to play, but he gets excessively zealous, as is his way. She has grown considerably but he's nearly twice as big as she is. When Keeley pounces on her Roo yowls and carries on – another tactic she learned from Dancer (and at which Cassie, and Marple before her, also excelled; is there something about the females of the species?). At any rate, it's an effective cease-and-desist signal.

Roo learned that, regarding Dancer, the aging matriarch was not likely to play with her (as all the cats had learned about Dancer), yet Dancer accepted Roo readily and didn't mind the young cat sitting closer to her than she allowed any of the others to do. Cassie, on the other hand, saw Roo as a rival at first, so Roo learned to stay out of her way. But when Cassie went through her personality changing ordeal with blindness and deafness, she warmed up to Roo at the same time. In Cassie's last months it was not unusual to see the two approach each other and touch noses in greeting.

There is one other thing that needs to be said about Roo. The greatest surprise of all was this: the ugly duckling has turned into a lovely swan. (Visitors to our house often want to take her home.) Underneath the stunted stray's homely scragginess and grungy, oddly patched fur lay a winsome beauty waiting to be released, a beauty of both looks and personality. She's a brown tabby (another one!), an attractive mix of brown, rust, cream, tan, black and gold. What had looked like ugly patches turned out, once she was clean and healthy, to be interesting patterns of stripes and patches in varying shades of black, brown and rust – with high concentrations of that lovely rust shade, a kind of burnt sienna color.

Now that she is no longer starving, Roo's head – and feet – look perfectly proportioned. Her forehead's tabby "M" is a two-tone affair, the outer legs of the M being rusty brown, the inner V being black. Multiple black stripes run from just behind the M, along her head, between her ears and onto her back. These elements give her an impossibly cute face: clear green eyes; a white chin; white whiskers whose roots are each surrounded by a black dot of fur; a medium brown, just slightly pugged nose. Ed insists she looks like W.C. Fields. (But then, he also says Digory's face looks like Yankee shortstop Derek Jeter. Strange as it sounds, he actually has a point.)

Roo's one souvenir from her unhappy days as a stray is a crook at the end of her tail where it was once broken. Perhaps it was stepped on; we hope it wasn't done deliberately. If it was, the memory of it for Roo appears to be long gone. She is now a charming, well-behaved cat (most of the time). Shortly after she arrived she startled us by snatching part of a pork chop off my dinner plate, literally right out from under my nose. She growled fiercely as she grabbed it – a signal to the other cats to keep away from her prize – then tore off down the hall to our bedroom, dragging the pork chop under the bed with her.

Roo

She's quick; she managed to do that a couple more times, with a chunk of hamburger and a slice of bacon. But gradually she learned that such is not acceptable behavior for a civilized cat. Of course she hadn't been civilized; or if she had, the people who thrust her from their lives when she was a kitten assured that in ousting her she would forget what she had learned.

As she came to realize that every single day, twice a day, a bowl of food would be set down in front of her – that she could rely on that happening without fail – she became less and less aggressive about her food (and mine, which she saw as hers if she could grab it before I ate it). Now, she waits patiently among her feline house mates if there is a meat scrap or two to be had. She waits eagerly though politely, too, for me to finish the dish of homemade yogurt I eat with almost every meal so that she can lick out the bowl. She relishes the yogurt, and is the only one who does. She lets out a little closed-mouth squeak of anticipation, but that's just the way she talks. She's a "talkative" cat and, to her mind, has a lot to talk about. She engages Ed and me in conversations every day but isn't at all perturbed when we don't appear to be brilliant enough to entirely understand her language.

She's no longer food-aggressive but that doesn't mean she doesn't love to eat. For a while she became, in fact, slightly too porky for her body size, so I began to watch her carefully at meal times so that when she had finished her own bowl she didn't head over to Digory's (or, previously, to Cassie's and/or Dancer's). Caspian and Keeley, had, months earlier, been banished to the bathroom during meals so that they could eat only their own food; they had decided, like Roo, that one helping of anything wasn't necessarily enough. Since Dancer and Cassie, nibblers both, are now gone, the three little pigs – Roo, Caspian and Keeley – have recently been welcomed back to the kitchen. Digory now needs to guard his food a little more closely, but (so far) they haven't dared bother Hedwig.

Roo is now past 3 ½ years old and thriving. Our rescue of her has allowed her to become the playful and happy cat God created cats to be. We literally saved her from death, and she has become, in her cat way, a wonderful example of contentment (and I would dare say of a kind of gratitude to us for saving her life). For us, she's an object lesson of complete trust.

We could not have guessed that the ugly little waif of a cat that we took in as an expensive charity case would blossom into a charming and feisty feline beauty, nor how dear to our hearts she would become.

Roo with Keeley, in their favorite window

8. Hedwig

Hedwig

Dancer's loss was still reverberating loudly. Then came Cassie's. That's when we discovered that four cats are *far* less than six. One-third less, mathematically speaking, but that difference seemed exponential. Little Roo was holding her own quite well with the three males, but the hole left by Dancer and Cassie seemed huge and deep. So I surprised myself when, not much more than a week after we buried Cassie, I began to yearn for another cat to add to the family. Thus, this story is ending very differently than I expected it would when I began writing it.

Our cat family being left with only one female, I reasoned that we should begin to look for a new female who needed a good home. But then Ed and I reminded each other of how negatively Roo had reacted to Patches, a young stray we had taken in for a few days the previous summer. I wasn't sure whether that was just Patches – who was self-confident and independent in the extreme – or whether it was because Patches was also female. In general, we've observed many time, females get along better with males than with other females.

I was uncertain what we should do and how soon we should do it. What egged me on, besides a renewed attack of cataholism, was that it was summer and the shelters were stuffed with unwanted cats born that spring, not to mention some older cats who had been abandoned or lost.

One afternoon I went to Lewiston to talk with the woman who

runs Niagara Feline Friends. We could certainly adopt one of their cats, if we wished, but it could be more crucial to get a cat from the Niagara County SPCA. The Feline Friends cats are guaranteed a place to live; they would never face execution for having been friendless. Not so with SPCA cats.

So my next stop was the Rainbow Shelter. I headed there with some apprehension, though I was just looking on that trip. And I wasn't entirely sure what I was looking *for*. I reminded myself that Dancer, Caspian and Keeley had all come from that shelter. And look how well that turned out!

I had a mere five minutes to look around before the shelter closed for the day. That was a good thing for a just-looking trip. I detest seeing cats in cages and I knew that, from a heart standpoint, I would want to take every one of them home.

I was taken aback by the number of kittens, young cats and a few older ones there. I had never seen it so crowded. I quickly perused both cat rooms and was greeted by insistent meows for attention and affection as I moved along the cages. By far the majority were young males in the three-to-six-months range. One pretty black-and-white five-year-old female had been "surrendered" by her family. I detected the grossest form of euphemism in that word and it made me blindly angry.

My heart went out to the cat; most people want kittens or cats under a year old. I tried to convince myself that perhaps the circumstances of that "surrender" were legitimate. I wondered whether a five-year-old cat would do well in our already established cat family.

There was another older cat that was morbidly obese (and she had already lost a full pound while on a diet in the shelter). That someone had allowed his or her cat to become that fat made me angrier still. *How can people unthinkingly, routinely, overfeed an animal they love?* I asked myself. Ah, but there was the rub: this cat clearly was not loved, or she would still have had a home.

There were several young females who called out to me and immediately engaged me. One young thing reminded me strongly of Delta; she had similar smoky blue-gray coloring, with bits of tan; a friendly, inquisitive little beauty. But one young male, an orange tabby, was the first to vie for my attention. He seemed a lively, likeable little guy. He, in fact, made me begin to rethink whether acquiring a female was the thing to do.

I told Ed that night at supper that I had visited the shelter, and what I had seen. A few days earlier I had brought up the subject of getting another cat. He wasn't against it by any means, but was in favor of waiting a bit longer. That was not an unreasonable approach. I argued, however, that it might be better to add a new one to the mix before Roo and the feline boys settled too deeply into new relationships among themselves, sans Cassie and Dancer.

That weekend, during our morning paper-reading session at breakfast I looked over the cat ads in our daily paper and in the regional freebie. I had been reconsidering whether we should adopt a shelter cat. It rankled me that they now charged twice as much as the no-kill shelters charged for adoption (and required cash), though the no-kill shelters also spayed or neutered, provided vaccinations and tested for several fatal diseases.

I called several numbers to inquire about cats advertised but got answering machines. When we received return calls we found out that several of the advertised cats were kittens and several were adult females.

I spoke at length with Beverly, a woman who, with her husband, fosters cats for Save-a-Pet, the organization from which Cassie had come. Their currently adoptable cats were an adult female, a couple of years old, two of her kittens, 14-weeks old, and a male about a year old. They all had been given names and it sounded clear that Beverly and her husband took good care of the cats in their charge. That became even more clear when we visited their home that afternoon some miles down the Lake Ontario shore.

Yes, that afternoon. The year-old male was a handsome orange tabby. He was friendly to Ed but entirely ignored me, and that didn't change during the half-hour we were there. The kittens were lively and playful, as healthy kittens are, but unheeding of the new human beings in the room. The two-year-old female, however, immediately trotted up to me and rubbed my legs. "I've never seen her do that to anyone else," said Beverly. I was pleased. Very pleased. The mother cat was an affectionate cat and tolerated a good deal of petting.

She was smoky gray with a small tan patch on her back, and tan feet. And she was rotund. Not obese, but several pounds overweight for the size of her frame, I estimated. That frame was very much the size Dancer had been (Cassie was smaller than Dancer). But her green-yellow eyes instantly reminded me of Cassie. Odd that this cat would look like a combination of the two cats we had just lost. That made me wary. Was I mentally transferring traits of Dancer's, and Cassie's too, onto this cat? She was an altogether different animal and should be related to on her own terms, I reminded myself.

Our hostess was calling the cat "Emma." Emma had come from a trailer park where she had been abandoned. As is so often the case with female strays, she was pregnant when rescued, presumably with her first litter, but that wasn't known for sure. She had been living with this Save-a-Pet family for more than four months, throughout her gestation and the birth and weaning of her kittens.

An odd thing had happened at that birth. She had had three kittens, accompanied by an unusual and alarming amount of blood, said Beverly. But she didn't actually hemorrhage and seemed to be all right. Sadly, though, two of the kittens was born dead. Two days later Emma suddenly lay down and birthed three remaining kittens, one of which also died. Now she needed a permanent home. It would fairly easy to find homes for her beautiful kittens – one was jet black with yellow eyes; one was a striking black-tinged tortoiseshell – but to find a good home for their rather porky two-year-old mother would be a bigger challenge.

Beverly and her husband left the room so that Ed and I could talk together. We soon came to a consensus. We would take the fat gray female (and immediately put her on a diet). In this case, we couldn't seriously fault her caregivers for her rotundity. They were caring for 15 or 16 cats which, as a practical matter, pretty much had to be allowed to graze at will. (And they were feeding their feline charges one of the highest quality dry foods available.) Allowing "grazing" works fine for cats who are nibblers, but those who aren't tend to gorge themselves, as we well knew from the natural habits of Caspian, Keeley and Roo.

I admit that "Emma" did not incite love at first sight in me, though I apparently did for her. For her own secret reasons, she immediately decided that I was hers. She was friendly and affectionate to Ed as well but it seemed that, to her mind, I had something special.

Our hostess was elated that we elected to adopt her. Beverly and her husband would bring Emma to our home around suppertime. It is

Hedwig

Save-a-Pet's policy that foster-carers bring an adopted animal to the new owner, no doubt so that they can get a look at the situation in which the cat will be living. That was fine with us. That would give me time to get the guest bedroom – cat holding cell that it would be once more – ready with a litter box, water bowl and towel bed. As always, we would keep the new cat in that room for a few days, both so that she would have a place of retreat away from the other cats and so that they could get used to her.

By late that evening we were already able to put a baby gate into the room's doorway so that the cats could all look at each other through the gate. (None of them thought to jump over it, as from experience we knew they likely wouldn't.)

As usual, Keeley tried to be friendly, wanting to touch noses with the gray, but she pushed him back with a hiss. Roo was initially fine as long as we petted her and assured her she would always be the Number One Spoiled Little Bugger of the Bunch, as she truly always will be. Digory was curious and even well-mannered, but astonishingly, Caspian's first move was to hiss at the intruding newcomer.

By Tuesday all feline parties were making good strides in getting used to each other, though the gray still spent time under the bed or in the laundry room behind the washer and dryer. That was not so strange, from her viewpoint. She was one against four, and an interloper – though we were pleased with how accepting the four already were of her. Occasionally in the next few weeks Roo would get jealous and take a run at the gray; or corner her, initiating a mutual growling fest. We suspected that might happen. But it would gradually subside as, thankfully, those things usually do.

What *was* curious is that Ed and I had a devil of a time coming up with a good name for the new girl. That had never happened before. Emma wasn't that "good name," in our view. That was partly because we have a niece whose daughter is Emma. (Cataholics that they, too, are, I doubt they would have minded if we usurped the name; but we declined.)

But what *would be* a good name? We tried Lucy – Lucy P. – after the feisty but good girl who is a main character in the *Narnia Chronicles*. That was a good idea, if only Lucy had been a name that we actually liked. It wasn't, we decided after a few days. There, too, it was a family member's name. My eldest sister, who died in an accident many years ago, was Lucille and her friends called her Lucy.

Then we hit on Hedwig, after Harry Potter's owl (spelled "Hedwig" not "Hedweg," as the name is usually spelled). Not unlike Dancer, this cat did indeed have large, owl-like eyes, and her round body of gray and tan fur added to the owl effect. Though Harry's owl was a snowy owl (and therefore white), we thought it seemed an appropriate name. But it had the potential to be a bit unwieldy and we did not want to shorten it to Heady. Because of that possible difficulty we wondered if Hedwig was really the right name.

So we started talking about names that aren't names, that is, names that are surnames or just words that have specific connotations, like Marple, Delta or Dancer. At breakfast on Tuesday Ed came up with "Dench," after the great British actress Judi Dench, whose skill we admire, who is short, and who for some roles has been rotund. It's a strong, solid name for a cat that has its wits about it, as this cat appears to. It seemed a good choice, yet as the day wore on I found myself gravitating back to Hedwig. Ed, as was his custom, had already found a variant on it: Hedwicker. It looked as if, at last, Hedwig it would be. A week later I had a name tag etched with the name and our phone numbers. The name had to stick! It has, and it has come to seem entirely appropriate. Ed, however, already has another nickname for Hedwig: Tilly. Here's his logic: it's short for Waltzing Matilda, which is the counterpart to Dancercat. Another relative of Stupe Naglia of Old's!

In just a few days I warmed up immensely to Hedwig. Though she was shy, she quickly began to show herself to be even more affectionate and good-natured than she had already appeared at first. But then – a setback; or two, actually.

After showing initial if somewhat hesitant friendliness to the other four cats, Hedwig began to retreat. She cowered and her eyes and body language showed fearfulness when she was around them. We didn't see any of them act aggressively toward her (though Roo did later), so we were mystified. We wondered again whether it had been a good idea to get an adult cat instead of a malleable, go-with-the-flow kitten or very young cat.

I telephoned Beverly. After a long talk, we both concluded that Hedwig would just need more time to adjust. She had been with us only a week, she had experienced various homes previously and had very likely been mistreated earlier in her life. She had gotten along all right with the many other cats at the foster home, though Beverly sensed that Hedwig was a cat that would do better in an environment with far fewer other cats – four, for instance.

Beverly mentioned a natural, flower-essence-based extract that works to reduce stress and that can be given to cats (as well as humans). Oddly enough, I had bought some of the very stuff about a month earlier, so began spraying some of it in Hedwig's water bowl every day. I can't say beyond a doubt that it helped, but she did seem to become a little more mellow and outgoing around the other cats, so perhaps it did.

A week-and-a-half after she arrived we still thought it best that she stay shut in the guest room overnight, giving her a safe place (and her own litter box, placed on plastic in a corner of the room) to be wholly herself during the night.

About that time I got up one morning to find that Digory – we *knew* it was Digory – had peed on the floor in the dining room (thankfully, not on the rug). The night before that he had "missed" the litter box, peeing on the vinyl mat outside one of the boxes, a mat meant to keep the litter from being tracked outside the Cat Bathroom.

He hadn't done such a thing in long time; but these were clearly deliberate acts. Despite spending the previous evenings on my lap and being given a great deal of attention, with Hedwig's arrival he was obviously feeling unsure of himself and his place in the group.

That night a thought suddenly occurred to me and Ed thought it was a good one: I would put Digory in the room with Hedwig for the night, making a bed for him on the old recliner in that room while Hedwig was in what was already a favorite spot on a towel bed placed on top of the desk in that room. We had found with previous cat introductions that that kind of strategy usually worked. The old cat and new cat could interact, or not, as they chose, learn things about each other and acclimatize to each other without interference from us.

Digory did well. He didn't meow to get out of the room, though early the next morning he was happy to come out. At that point, about 5:30 a.m., I put Caspian in the room instead and Ed let both him and Hedwig out when he got up.

That afternoon, Hedwig joined the others in my office, sitting on one of the filing cabinets with a strategic view of the bird feeder and the squirrels, chipmunks and sparrows busily scurrying after seeds there. The night before, Ed had said, "Maybe someday we'll look back on this and think, 'How could we ever have even considered bringing Hedwig back. She may turn out to be a wonderful cat like Roo." I smiled. I had been thinking exactly the same thing. I told Ed so. That happened frequently, and not just related to the cats. It was pleasant to know that we were united in our reaction to Hedwig. One thing is for sure, she's a *quiet* cat, a self-contained creature, as many would say cats should be. The only exception would soon start to occur at mealtimes. As she felt more at home she began, twice a day, to serenade us urgently for a half minute or so as she watched me dish out the cat food. I take it to mean, "Don't forget *me!*" – which of course I never will. She will some day understand that, I'm sure.

As we were all overcoming that first setback, a second one suddenly revealed itself one morning. Three weeks after her arrival we awoke to find Hedwig lying in meatloaf position, her sides quivering oddly. She ate only a few bites then lay on her towel on the couch all morning and afternoon. She was in pain – she growled when carried -- and her abdomen was bloated. Placing a hand gently on her belly seemed to ease her discomfort. I called Beverly to ask whether such a thing had ever arisen before. It hadn't, at least not while Hedwig was in Beverly's care. We both concluded that it might be gas.

It was, but it was more. By late afternoon she had not improved so I called Dr. Downey's office. That evening, x-rays showed a large accumulation of feces in her colon. The poor cat was gaseous and constipated, though the reason wasn't apparent. Possibly the rather shy cat was stressed and that's how her body reacted to the tension. After a lengthy discussion with Dr. D.'s associate, who was working that evening, we went home with a laxative. By the next morning, and a dose-and-a-half downed, Hedwig was slightly lighter – and feeling noticeably better. And each following day she improved.

We will do whatever we can to help her spend the rest of her days as a healthy and happy cat. All in all, she has been adjusting well; both Ed and I were perhaps a little impatient with her at first. I think I had not allowed myself to fully commit to taking in an adult cat.

As each day passes Hedwig is becoming more openly affectionate and, bit by bit, more self-assured and playful. It turns out that, like Roo, she has an innate attraction to "hockey" played with plastic sealing rings from vitamin bottles; and she' good at it. In revealing that talent she has also revealed a hitherto mostly hidden source of energy and fun. (Recently, when that talent surfaced, Roo seemed nonplussed as she watched Hedwig; she wanted to join the game but was unsure how Hedwig would respond.)

Hedwig is showing us new reasons to love her. She is also proving that she can hold her own at chow time, and that she loves that time each day (twice) as much as Caspian, Keeley and Roo do. She's never late to the kitchen!

We're convinced that she will be a fine addition to our feline family; and that the rest of that family will soon think so too.

Postscript: Patches and Thousands More

Early in 2008, two young strays arrived in the neighborhood. That's uncommon here. They were obviously good buddies, probably male and female litter-mates who found their way to our street after being dumped by yet another heartless supposed animal lover. The young pair, a calico and a brown tabby, were wary of people but were not feral. They began to routinely slink through our yard on their rounds, whose route only they knew for sure. Our neighbor across the street and her daughter, who each have a cat themselves, set out food for the pair now and then. So did someone down the street.

Then the tabby disappeared, having met an ill end, we sadly imagined. The calico seemed lost without him but she continued to hang around and got bolder and friendlier. She discovered that with at least some residents that kind of charm worked to get herself a meal.

Patches

I started seeing the calico at odd times during the day when previously she and her brother would lie low most days and come by at dusk or early morning. I called to her on one of those occasions. I was surprised when she ran up to me. I sat down on our front porch. She was a little skittish but gradually sidled up the walk toward me, then sat down next to me. She let me stroke her. I was elated that she trusted me.

She was hungry. I went to the garage, poured out some dry food and put it in a plastic bowl for her near the side of the house. I continued to do that every day. Some days I didn't see her but the food would disappear. Some days she would come by and consent to be petted. I called her Patches because of the calico patches – white, black, rust, tan – all over her body.

I wondered if she had already been spayed. She was surely old enough to be pregnant and did not appear to be. That she wasn't pregnant was confirmed by September when she was still coming around and remained her thin, now friendly self.

Ed didn't mind me feeding Patches, though he was certain that we should not, just then, take on, or in, another cat on any permanent basis. (We still had our six.) It had been just a year since we had adopted Roo – the result of my only other foray into feeding a stray. This time, I didn't think he'd be swayed with the argument, "And look how well that turned out!" Six cats were enough, I fully agreed. But Patches needed a home. By default I would be the one in our neighborhood to spearhead the effort to find her one.

I called our friend Paula, who feeds our cats when we go on vacation. Could I convince her to take Patches? She already had one cat but lives in a small apartment and was concerned about how her fairly elderly cat would react. Then, too, vet bills would be prohibitive just then. We then asked an older friend who has one cat, a stray she had taken in. She had lost a second cat recently to illness. She agreed to take Patches. I was relieved. But I detected some apprehension in her voice. She might need an out. "Try it," I suggested, "and if it doesn't work I'll take her back."

Patches wreaked havoc and fought with the existing cat. Our friend was up all night trying to referee. I drove to Lewiston to retrieve Patches, then put her in our garage (lately it had been cold and rainy). Next we moved her into the guest room while I was still looking for a final home for her. I had grown attached to her but I knew it just wouldn't work to keep her, and Ed strongly seconded that sentiment. Roo would have none of it.

Forgetting where she herself had come from, Roo growled and hissed possessively to keep Patches at bay and was in a generally morose mood unlike we had ever seen her display. This was *her* home! *What was this intruder doing here?*

Three days passed and Roo had become downright despondent. Ed was upset on Roo's behalf. I, too, was uneasy about Roo's response but I was reluctant to bring Patches to the shelter. I felt again as I had felt when we found Roo: What if no one adopted her?

I had mentioned Patches on the previous Wednesday night at my church-choir rehearsal. A pair of choir members, married to each other, have two young children who had been yearning for a cat. As I seriously began to wonder how to get out of the mess I'd gotten myself into, they told me they would take Patches. *Yee hah!* My prayers were answered, I was out of trouble and would soon be back in Roo's good graces. Within half a year, the family who took Patches adopted a second kitten, another from among the millions that need homes.

Not long ago, Paula – fellow cataholic – was regularly seeing a long-haired orange tabby near her apartment. She named him Giorgio. She told me about him and again considered whether she should take on a second cat. She was torn, for the same reasons as before, but it was clear to me that she had a soft spot for this particular cat. In the end, she decided to go ahead.

We took Giorgio to Dr. Downey's clinic to get him checked out. He was already neutered and an ear tattoo told of his having been, at some time in his young life, in a shelter in Buffalo. Paula had been looking in the usual places for notices of a lost orange tabby but saw nothing to indicate that he was now a loved pet who was missed and being looked for.

Giorgio has adjusted well to his new surroundings, as his housemates, human and feline, have to him – and as I was sure they would. Knowing how much our cats love Paula (she *plays* with them as well as feeds them when we're gone!), I know he's going to have a good life. Such an ending makes any cat lover happy.

Ed and I have been able, so far, to provide a home for ten cats and have helped save a couple of others along the way. For those ten, who have immeasurably enriched our lives, being adopted was a life and death matter, as it is for as many as three million cats a year which face euthanasia. Picture that number, if you can. The great majority of those are not so fortunate as our ten have been; being ousted from a home or born on the street or in a field is far too often an early death sentence.

I'm contemplating another "cat project." I want to embark on a mission to get my town, and then the one next door, and then the next one and those throughout the county to require the registration of all cats by the time they are three months old; and to require that all such cats be spayed or neutered. Shelters require spaying or neutering in order to adopt cats. But pet shops do not. Somehow thousands of people still have sexually intact cats which they allow to breed. And then they don't know what to do with the hundreds of thousands of resulting kittens. The majority are euthanized (or die in far more gruesome and painful circumstances). Our legal system, too, seldom appropriately penalizes people who treat living, intelligent animals as if they are inanimate things that can be put out with the garbage.

All those homeless cats running loose naturally need to find food for themselves. But an additional problem – and it's serious – is the havoc they wreak on the already depleting songbird population (not to mention other animals they kill).

If all cats either had imbedded microchips containing their ID and owner's information or wore a collar and ID tag with a registration number (as dogs generally must), the problem of wandering cats of unknown origin would be greatly diminished. At the very least it would help immensely to find cats that escape from their homes and get lost. Currently only 10 percent of such animals are reunited with their owners. Some cities, notably Denver, are providing free cat microchip services to help alleviate that problem. Other cities need to be urged to follow suit, or to do so for a minimal fee.

If you're in a position to offer a good home to one or several cats, consider visiting your local shelter or taking in a stray. So far we've done it nine times (with one home-grown).

"And look how well that turned out!"

The End

(Keeley, Caspian, Digory: waiting to see the vet.)

If you enjoyed this book (or even if you didn't) and wish to contact the author, email her via *Cataholic@wordpowerpublishing.com.*

Or: <www.WordPowerPublishing.com> will direct you to Marian's Cataholic blog, where you may publicly comment on this book, get updates on the author's cats, or tell your own cat tales.

Breinigsville, PA USA
22 October 2009
226319BV00001B/4/P